DARING TO DREAM BIG
UNLEASHING YOUR INNER COURAGE

DR VALARIE W. HARRIS

STEPPING OUT
WITH PURPOSE

Daring to Dream Big: Unleashing Your Inner Courage

Copyright © 2024 Dr. Valarie W. Harris

Scripture quotations marked (NIV) are taken from THE HOLY BIBLE, NEW INTERNATIONAL VERSION®. Copyright© 1973, 1978, 1984, 2011 by Biblica, Inc.™. Used by permission of Zondervan.

Scripture quotations marked (KJV) are taken from the KING JAMES VERSION, public domain.

Scripture quotations marked (NKJV) are taken from the NEW KING JAMES VERSION®. Copyright© 1982 by Thomas Nelson, Inc. Used by permission. All rights reserved.

Scriptures marked ESV are taken from THE HOLY BIBLE, ENGLISH STANDARD VERSION (ESV): Scriptures taken from THE HOLY BIBLE, ENGLISH STANDARD VERSION ® Copyright© 2001 by Crossway, a publishing ministry of Good News Publishers. Used by permission.

Scriptures marked NLT are taken from the HOLY BIBLE, NEW LIVING TRANSLATION (NLT): Scriptures taken from the HOLY BIBLE, NEW LIVING TRANSLATION, Copyright© 1996, 2004, 2007 by Tyndale House Foundation. Used by permission of Tyndale House Publishers, Inc., Carol Stream, Illinois 60188. All rights reserved. Used by permission.

Published by
Stepping Out with Purpose™
www.steppingoutwithpurpose.com

Anthology Editor
Chandra Sparks Splond, M.S.E.
www.chandrasparkssplond.com

Book Creation and Design

Brand It Beautifully™
www.branditbeautifully.com

Photographer
Kimie James
www.IYQphotography

ISBN for Paperback version: ISBN: 979-8-9877190-6-0
ISBN for Hardcover version: 979-8-9877190-7-7
ISBN for Digital version: 979-8-9877190-8-4

Printed in the United States of America

DEDICATION

To the dreamers, the doers, and the believers:
This book is a special token of appreciation dedicated. May you find
the courage to chase your dreams, the strength to overcome any
obstacle, and the wisdom to embrace the journey of self-discovery
and growth. Your potential is limitless, and the world needs your
unique brilliance. Thank you for daring to dream big and allowing
this book to be a part of your inspiring journey.

TABLE OF CONTENTS

FOREWORD
MALINDA WILLIAMS

In *The Wizard of Oz*, the Cowardly Lion sought just "a bit of courage." He believed he was not fulfilling his purpose as king of the beasts because he felt he lacked the innate courage, strength, and power required. Little did the Cowardly Lion know that the courage he sought was already within him, just waiting to be unleashed.

Dr. Valarie Harris, my dear cousin, mentor, and friend, is a visionary who understands that sometimes we all need a little help to realize our inner courage. Unleashing that courage requires more than just a special elixir. It requires the guidance, support, and wisdom of someone like Dr. Val, who is an advocate for all of us, encouraging us to be the best version of ourselves.

As a teenager, whenever Valarie visited us, she never failed to go out of her way to make each visit special for her younger cousins. Today, she continues to do something special for others, and I am consistently amazed by the energy and heart she pours into every endeavor. Whether it is working tirelessly on mission trips to Ghana, West Africa; writing; hosting seminars and focused videos; serving in her church; managing speaking engagements; or mentoring others, Dr. Val exemplifies what it means to be a servant leader. She has a particular passion for encouraging, empowering, and educating women, and I witnessed firsthand how she has taken women under her wing, helping them to flourish and reach their highest potential. Her passion and love shine through in the strong bonds she forms, as she is surrounded by authentic friends and women who share her mission. The camaraderie within her circle is truly worthy of admiration and emulation.

As a lifelong educator, associate minister, director of ministries, empowerment coach, leadership consultant, magazine contributor, author of nine books, and the inspiration behind four collaborative works, Dr. Val has consistently lived out her purpose. Her dedication to this labor of love is evident in the time, energy, wisdom, and expertise she has shared with Erika, Marilyn, Zelda, and me. We are immensely grateful for Dr. Val, for this opportunity that has brought us together, and for the enduring relationships we now cherish.

From her first book, *Talk Time with God*, to now, Dr. Val has poured her heart into every publication, and we have all done the same in this collaborative effort. Thank you, Dr. Val, for inspiring us throughout this journey. While this collaboration centers on a single theme, we offer wisdom from various perspectives, ensuring that every reader will find something that resonates with them on a profound and lasting level.

I urge you to delve into these pages and find what speaks to you, something that will help you harness the courage needed to walk confidently into your purpose and make your dreams a reality. In his instructions to the Thessalonians, the Apostle Paul urged them to love each other "more and more," and in the same way, the challenges of today's world call for us to follow Dr. Val's example—we must increasingly encourage one another. Just as kindness is contagious, so is encouragement. Together, we can witness the powerful ripple effect of others daring to dream big, unleashing their inner courage, and achieving tremendous success.

INTRODUCTION

Welcome to a transformative journey that begins with a single, powerful decision—the decision to dream big. In a world where we often find ourselves confined by societal expectations, self-doubt, and the fear of failure, daring to dream beyond the boundaries of the ordinary is an act of courage. Start expressing that your life's meant for more impact, purpose, and fulfillment.

This book, *Daring to Dream Big: Unleashing Your Inner Courage,* is not just about achieving success. Discover the greatness within you that has been waiting to be unleashed. It's about embracing the boldness to step out of your comfort zone, to challenge the limitations that have held you back, and to walk in the fullness of your potential. Your dreams are not just fleeting thoughts; they are seeds of possibility, planted within you by a divine purpose, waiting to grow into a life that serves you and inspires and empowers others.

As you turn the pages, you will find stories, insights, and strategies from women who have dared to dream big—women like you who have faced obstacles but chose to rise above them. Their journeys will inspire you to embrace your path with courage and conviction. You will learn how to cultivate the mindset and habits necessary to overcome fear, take bold steps forward, and manifest the life you've always envisioned.

Remember, this is your time. You are not here by accident; you are here because you are ready to unleash your inner courage and step into the life you were destined to live. Let's embark on this empowering journey of self-discovery, growth, and transformation together. Let's dare to dream big—and make those dreams a reality. As you turn these pages, remember that you can change your story.

Your journey starts now.

MANIFESTING DREAMS INTO REALITY

ERIKA N. BROOKS, LPC, CSAC

In January 2020, I attended a vision board workshop. Now, I have created vision boards in the past, so I thought I knew what to expect—cutting and pasting some images and words of how I was going to lose weight, live a healthier life, spend more time getting closer to God, and spending time with family. But this experience was different. This wasn't a "regular" vision board workshop. This two-day event was led by two women who felt the call from God to gather women together to manifest their thoughts, prayers, and plans for the calendar year.

Before the workshop, we had been encouraged to think about what we wanted for the upcoming year and how we wanted God to show up in our lives. During the first meeting, we talked about our spiritual gifts and how we tap into them. We also discussed prayers and how we manifest them. We also talked about hearing His directions for our lives. The second day, we created our boards—what I will be referring to as our manifestation boards. As my fellow workshop participants were busy at work, I found myself stuck. I didn't know what to put down and didn't know what God wanted me to do. I knew that being a therapist is where He wanted me serving His people, but what else was I to do?

As I sat at the table and looked at my sisters around me working and finding words and images that they felt spoke to their next steps, I quietly wept because I felt I wasn't hearing from God. To avoid feeling like I wasted this time, I started clipping images that represented what I wanted 2020 to be about. Images of the beach, family, and friendship soon filled my board. Phrases such as *Watch the Throne* and *Self-Care 2.0* spoke to me. And then I found two that I was drawn to: *Have Fresh Dreams* and *When I Dream in Black, I Step in My Reality*. They were ordinary and simple words, and I could not understand why they were speaking so loudly to me, but I would soon understand and learn how to manifest my dreams into my reality.

DARE TO DREAM A LITTLE DREAM

When I left the workshop, I felt very lost, so I prayed for clarity and understanding. I took my board home and put it in my office. I didn't frame it right away because I didn't feel connected to any of it. After a few days, I decided to get to work. Since the word *dream* kept creeping up on my vision board, I decided to do a little research to help me understand what I was supposed to be learning/gaining and how I was going to be obedient to these words. I knew I had always had dreams, especially about family and friends, but I didn't think they meant anything other than the dream was because I had been thinking of that person and/or how much fun we would have together.

We all have dreams. Sometimes they are good. Sometimes they are bad (or nightmares). But what are dreams really, and how do they happen? Well, there are a couple different meanings of the word. According to *Merriam-Webster, dream* can be a person or thing that is perceived as wonderful or perfect. It can also be a cherished aspiration, ambition, or ideal. A dream is "a series of thoughts, images, and sensations occurring in a person's mind during sleep." This often occurs in REM (rapid eye movement) sleep.

Now, to give you a little science/biology, when we sleep, we go through two different levels of sleep, REM and non-rapid eye movement (NREM). Experts break down NREM sleep in three different substages—N1, N2, and N3. As we sleep, we cycle through all these stages. Typically, we tend to have longer, deeper REM sleep near morning hours or our wake time.

To put in context how our bodies work in these stages, think of it like this: N1 is the falling asleep/light sleep zone. Our heartbeat and breathing are slowing down, and our body is relaxing. We are barely asleep but still can wake up easily. It's that "I must have drifted off" during a commercial break kind of sleep. N2 sleep is still a light sleep, but we're beginning to enter deep sleep. Our breathing is slower than in N1, and our eyes aren't moving. This is the stage where we spend most of our sleep. It's a little harder to wake us up—we can still arouse easily. With N3, our breath and heartbeat are slow, no eye movement, and we are completely relaxed. This is the time we get restorative sleep. Our brain is busy strengthening our immune system, repairing our weary muscles and cells. This is what I like to refer to as the "I was knocked out" phase. We are not easily awakened at this stage.

In REM sleep, there are two phases. The first is phasic REM sleep in which our eyes will move in quick (rapid) bursts. In tonic REM sleep, there is no eye movement. In REM stage, there is increased brain activity, breathing, and heart rate. This normally begins about ninety minutes after falling asleep. From research, experts stated that most people spend about two hours a night dreaming in this stage. Now, keep in mind, we can and often do dream in the NREM stages, *but* our most vivid dreams (and the ones we remember) often occur during REM sleep.

Along with my research, I learned that we cannot "create" our dreams, but our lifestyle behaviors can affect how and what we dream. I learned that what we eat and the time we eat can affect what we dream. Remember the episode of *The Cosby Show* where Dr. Huxtable ate the sub late at night before bed, and he dreamed that the men in the family gave birth to things like a toy car and submarine sandwich? Yes, eating heavy food late at night can trigger poor sleep, which in turn can trigger negative or disturbing dreams. Other factors that can contribute to negative dreams include stress, anxiety, alcohol/drug use, illness, and medication. External factors include the temperature of the room, noise, and comfort of the sleeping space.

For me, I know that I dream (thinking of what to do, obtain) during my dreams (while I am sleep). I also know that for me, dreams are often messages from God and often reveal things that I need to know or do.

DON'T WAKE ME...I'M DREAMING

With this knowledge in mind, I decided to learn as much as I could about my dreams. I started writing down my dreams—the good and the bad ones. There were dreams in which I saw myself in therapy sessions, which made sense to me. There were dreams where I was in a group of people talking about life events. These types of dreams seemed normal and, quite frankly, ordinary. But then there were times I would dream about running a program working with girls and having different groups and dreams about speaking to an auditorium of people, which absolutely terrified me. I kept a notebook beside my bed (and still do) so I could l write anything that came up in my sleep. I did my best to write as soon as I woke up because I felt like my memory was freshest then. I wrote down every detail—people, places, things—even what felt like minute details. I also would write questions or my thoughts as to why I had that particular dream. In the beginning, I was using sticky notes, but I realized the experts were right, we do dream a lot, so I got a notebook and made sure to keep all the sticky notes.

Now, there were some days that I did not write much of anything, but there were days when I dreamed of activities and programs that I was leading. Some of these dreams were alarming because they were things outside of my comfort zone or things I had no idea how to make happen. I would write them down, but in the back of my mind, I tried to write them off. But if you are a believer in Christ, you know that when there is a task for you to do, He will not let you run from it. I kept those dreams in the notebook, and as I continued my writings, I began to realize what the *Have Fresh Dreams* on my board meant.

Along with writing, I would pray for understanding and clarity of my dreams. Prayer has always been especially important in my life because I truly believe that God is the head and leader of my life. I believe that my dreams—good or bad—are from Him, and whatever direction I go in in life is led by Him. I also had been told that I receive my messages from God in my dreams. I began to talk to my aunt, who is a minister, who sometimes gave me clarity about aspects of a dream from a spiritual standpoint. She also prayed with and for me to gain clarity, understanding, and wisdom to know what I was to gain from my dreams. I also asked my friends and family to pray with me and for me in understanding and obedience because honestly, I was seeing that the dreams were becoming a blueprint.

HOW I TURNED MY DREAMS INTO MY REALITY

Unfortunately, two months after the workshop, the world was down due to the COVID pandemic. Fortunately, this time of confinement to home gave me the time to dedicate to making my dreams a reality. Because we could not go out, but the demand for mental health services increased, I brought my counseling business home and provided outpatient therapy virtually. I also began to provide some couples sessions and to develop more of a presence on social media. I created a business to share information about maintaining one's mental health during the pandemic. I began to accept invitations to share my knowledge. I was gaining clients, making a mark in the mental health world. I was following my dream of helping

God's people through my form of ministry—counseling. I realized that I was following the blueprint God had for my life and was sharing through my dreams. I was happy with what I was doing, but remember, I said earlier some of those dreams can be scary and will move you outside of your comfort zone?

I have always had the gift of gab, which is why I honestly believe I was meant to be a therapist. As the world slowly started opening back up after the pandemic, I began to attend workshops and conferences to expand my mental health business. I was providing sessions, but I knew not everyone was going to be willing or able to attend therapy, so I began researching other ways to provide the information and care. In regard to that dream of talking to groups of people, I participated and appeared on various podcasts and even spoke at a live event for women and talked about mental health and self-care. I also became an author, contributing to an anthology and a women's magazine. I also was invited to speak at a conference for women business professionals as well as to present my own workshop sessions to spiritual leaders about trauma and the church.

DREAM ON, DREAMER

There have been so many lessons I have learned from my dreams, and it has been a true blessing to be able to manifest them into reality. Here are some things you can do to learn and manifest from your dreams.

- **Capture your dreams.** No, I am not referring to a dream catcher, although they are nice and hold importance to certain groups. What I mean is record your dreams, whether it be by writing or recording. When you wake up and remember a dream, write it down—or better yet, record it on your phone or recorder. Write as much detail as you can. Where were you in your dream? Who was with you? What was happening? Why were you where you were in the dream? What was going on in the dream—has it happened before? Also note if you have had this dream before. I have found that often my dreams make no sense to me in that moment, but later on, they develop into something.

When it comes to your dreams/goals, make sure to be specific. Clearly define what you want to achieve/gain. The more specific you are with your vision, the easier it is to focus your energy/thoughts and take the necessary steps to reach it. Write down what you want. What does that look like? What will that feel like when you attain it? Why do these goals/dreams matter to you?

- **Ask for guidance.** Talk to God or your Higher Power, and ask for guidance, understanding, and patience. Often, the dream is not clear, but with time and patience, we can understand what it means and what we are to do. I have conversations with God daily, and sometimes, those conversations are messages of gratitude for His guidance to the point where I have made it. Honest conversations with your Higher Power will guide your steps, connect you with the right people, and move you further on the journey.
- **Create a vision board.** Having a vision board/goal board gives you a visual aid to reinforce any goals or

dreams you have. Make sure to place this somewhere you will see on a daily basis to keep your mind on your goals and keep you on track. Although my vision board was created in 2020, it still has a lot of images and words that are still goals for me, and I don't think that I have completed all of those dreams God has for me.

- **Set your intentions.** Setting an intention involves a firm commitment to achieving your dream. It is backed with purpose and determination. Break down your dream into small, manageable goals/steps. This will help make the journey less overwhelming and less fearful. It will also help you to track your progress and note the success toward the dreams.

- **Take consistent action.** I admit that some days are harder than others to devote time to your goals/dreams when you have other obligations. It is important for you to develop daily habits and routines to get you to your goals. Each step, no matter how big or small, is getting you to your dreams. Each day, plan to work on your dreams. Learn new skills, new techniques, or simply plan the next step.

- **Stay committed.** Staying committed to your dreams even when it feels unattainable is key. Challenges will come, but look at them as a chance to grow and learn. Let the challenges push you further to your dreams.

- **Celebrate the big and small steps.** Remember, reaching your dreams is not going to happen overnight. It is a process, so enjoy every moment of the way. Celebrate the big and the small steps along the way. Be grateful for the progress you make. Take moments to be grateful for the things you learn along the journey, which will help to keep a positive mindset. You may also take time to celebrate those who have been on the journey with you and/or who joined along the way.

- **Reflect and adjust.** Throughout the journey, take time to review progress and reflect on what's working and what is not. Adjust your plans as needed to continue on the journey to reaching your dreams.

- **Embrace new opportunities.** I never had an idea I wanted to write or that I would love it so much. It opened me up to the opportunity when I began working with a business coach, and I have been able to attract a different audience outside of my therapy sessions. Writing has allowed me a new venue to reach and teach about mental health for those who normally come in contact with me. Keep your mind open to new possibilities that align with your dreams. Sometimes opportunities that you never imagined may come in unexpected forms. You have to be open-minded to recognize and seize them.

- **Face your fears.** It is important to acknowledge any fears and/or doubts that arise and address them immediately. Spend some time thinking about what is holding you back and create ways to overcome these concerns. It is up to you how you define F.E.A.R.—*Fear Everything and Run* or *Face Everything and Rise.*

- **Embrace the mistakes.** I learned from watching Bob Ross, a painter who used to have television shows that taught you how to paint. When he made a mistake, he always turned it into what he called a "happy little ending." So, if he was creating something like a flower, and it was a little off, he may turn it into a "happy little" tree. The point is, turn the mistake into something nice. Do not be afraid to learn from the experience as it will bring you closer to the dream.

- **Build your support network.** Surround yourself with people who are going to encourage, inspire, and support you. These should be people who support your dreams. A good support network will assist you with advice, encouragement, and even knowledge for the journey. Do not forget to include groups or organizations that may be able to give guidance as they have attained similar goals. Seek support and be valuable in saving your time and effort.
- **Stay connected to your why.** Throughout the journey, remind yourself why you are pursuing this dream. Keeping your motivation and passion will help you through challenges and keep you focused on your ultimate goals.

Whatever your dream, wherever it takes you, enjoy the journey and never be afraid to dream fresh dreams.

MEET THE AUTHOR | ERIKA N. BROOKS, LPC, CSAC

Erika N. Brooks is a dynamic force in the world of mental health, radiating passion and dedication in every facet of her work. As a Licensed Professional Counselor (LPC) and Certified Substance Abuse Counselor (CSAC) in Virginia, Erika's expertise is backed by a master of science in rehabilitation counseling from Virginia Commonwealth University. She is the proud owner of Enlightenment Counseling Services, LLC, where she tirelessly champions women's health, mental well-being, self-care, trauma recovery, and grief therapy.

Erika's influence stretches far beyond her counseling office. She is a celebrated voice on various podcasts, where she dives deep into discussions about mental health and self-care, particularly within the African-American community. Her insights and empathetic approach have made her a sought-after guest and a beacon of support for many.

In an exciting development, Erika is working on her own podcast, *TEA Time with Erika.* set to become a go-to resource for anyone looking to improve their mental health and embrace self-care. Additionally, her literary contributions are nothing short of inspiring. Erika is a co-author of the transformative books *PEARL: Wisdom and Advice for Emerging Leaders* and *Positioned to Pivot,* offering guidance and inspiration to aspiring leaders everywhere. She also enriches the pages of *Hope Magazine for Women* with her insightful articles.

Erika's commitment to healing and growth extends to her role as a board member for Forever Healed, a for-profit organization dedicated to supporting individuals through grief and loss. Here, she provides outpatient therapy, bringing her compassionate expertise to those in need.

Her community involvement is equally impressive. Erika is an active member of the National Coalition of 100 Black Women, where she works to empower Black women and girls. Her dedication to her church and local community further highlight her unwavering commitment to service and support.

In her personal life, Erika embodies the principles she teaches. She cherishes time with her family and friends, loves reading, and is a steadfast advocate for self-care.

Erika is not just a counselor; she is a vibrant leader, a compassionate healer, and a relentless advocate for mental health and empowerment. Her work continues to light the way for countless individuals striving for better mental health and a brighter future.

YOUR THOUGHTS

_____

_____

_____

_____

_____

_____

_____

_____

_____

_____

_____

_____

_____

_____

_____

_____

_____

_____

_____

_____

_____

_____

YOUR THOUGHTS

NURTURED BY LOVE, FUELED BY CHALLENGES

DR. VALARIE W. HARRIS

I was fortunate to grow up as an only child in Newport News, Virginia, with two caring parents who worked hard to support me despite our difficulties. My mother worked tirelessly as a crab processor at the marina in Hampton, Virginia, and my father was a Langley Field Air Force Base rigger. We lived a simple life in the projects, but my home was filled with love, resilience, and the values that shaped the person I am today.

It was a time when your neighborhood was your village, where you could walk to school without fear of violence or disrespect. I remember the strong sense of community, the support of our neighbors, and the security of knowing that we looked out for one another. But, like many families, we also faced our share of disappointments and challenges.

My father, despite his struggles with alcohol, was a great provider. His presence and work ethic taught me early on about persistence. I saw in my father the resilience to keep going and work hard despite personal battles. But it wasn't just my father's perseverance that shaped my understanding of persistence—my mother was a living example of it, too.

My mother didn't get her driver's license until about age thirty-nine. Until then, she caught the bus to work every day, never complaining or letting it deter her from providing for our family. Watching her rise early, face the day with determination, and handle her responsibilities with grace left a deep impression on me. Her persistence and robust work ethic showed me that no matter what obstacles stand in your way, you can always find a way to move forward.

Both of my parents exemplified the kind of persistence and resilience that became the foundation of my understanding that persistence is essential when daring to dream big, no matter the challenges. They demonstrated through their actions that hard work, consistency, and never give up pushing toward your dreams, no matter how difficult the journey may be.

Prayer became my anchor during those formative years. As a child, I often turned to God in times of uncertainty, asking for guidance and strength. Growing up with obstacles, I learned that prayer was more than a ritual—it was a lifeline that helped me keep faith in a brighter future. I leaned on prayer to keep me grounded and connected to a vision for my life, even when the path forward wasn't clear.

Through prayer, I discovered my passion for education and leadership. I wasn't just dreaming of escaping the simple life we lived in the projects—I was dreaming of a future where I could make a difference for myself and others. I knew that education was the key, and that passion fueled my every decision. The obstacles we faced as a family didn't hold me back—they ignited a fire in me to push beyond those limitations.

Discovering my purpose began in childhood, nurtured by the love of my parents and the close-knit community around me. Initially, it wasn't always clear, but I began to understand that my purpose involved empowering others to step out of their comfort zones, just as I had to do. My purpose gave me a sense of direction and a reason to dream big despite the setbacks.

Growing up in the projects, I often felt the weight of limited resources, but my parents taught me to always believe in my potential. They reminded me that I could achieve great things and that my circumstances didn't define me. This belief in my potential was a driving force behind every goal I set for myself. I knew there was more to life than what I saw around me, and I was determined to reach it.

Of course, the journey wasn't without its challenges. Persistence became my greatest ally. I watched my parents work hard daily despite our struggles, and their perseverance became my example. I realized early on that success doesn't come overnight and that I would need to keep pushing forward, no matter how difficult the road ahead seemed.

But persistence alone isn't enough. I also learned the importance of preparation. As a child, I prepared for a future beyond the projects by focusing on my education and seeking mentors who could guide me. I took every opportunity to learn, grow, and equip myself with the tools I needed to succeed. Preparation transforms dreams into reality, and I was committed to doing the work.

Throughout it all, maintaining a positive mindset was crucial. It would have been easy to become discouraged by our circumstances or to allow fear and doubt to take over. But I chose to see the possibilities instead of the limitations. My parents' love and our community's strength helped me cultivate a mindset of hope and determination. I believed that if I could dream it, I could achieve it.

These pillars—prayer, passion, purpose, potential, persistence, preparation, and a positive mindset—were critical in my journey from a little girl in Newport News, Virginia, to the empowered woman I am today. They guided me as I dared to dream big and pursue a life beyond the expectations others had for me.

Looking back now, I see that every obstacle and disappointment shaped me for a greater purpose. My journey wasn't just about reaching personal success—it was about creating a legacy that would inspire others to dream big, rise above their circumstances, and live out their God-given purpose.

So, when I speak about daring to dream big, I'm not just talking about the power of ambition but the power of transformation. It's about using every setback as a stepping stone and every challenge as an opportunity to grow. It's about leaning into your faith, trusting your potential, and never losing sight of your dreams, no matter where you start.

As my journey in life moved forward from elementary school, where I learned the values of independence and self-reliance, I carried those lessons into high school. There, I found a new passion—playing the cello in the school orchestra. Music became a creative outlet that balanced my academic life and helped me develop discipline, focus, and teamwork. These qualities served me well as I navigated the challenges and joys of my teenage years.

As I transitioned to college, I started as a business major, following a more conventional path. But something within me wasn't delighted. I felt that there was a more profound calling that involved making a more direct impact on the lives of others. I shifted my focus to working with children with disabilities, and that change felt like coming home to a purpose that was meant for me. Working with those children was rewarding in ways I never imagined. It wasn't just about teaching; it was about helping them discover their potential and witnessing the incredible resilience they showed every day. Even though I was still figuring things out, I knew I was on the right path.

Once I graduated from college, I stepped into my career as a teacher with excitement and a sense of mission. The classroom became my canvas, where I could use my gifts to empower young minds. I quickly realized that teaching wasn't just about lessons and grades—it was about building relationships, fostering confidence, and helping my students recognize their capabilities, no matter their challenges.

This new chapter of my life brought obstacles, but each was an opportunity to apply the seven pillars that had guided me since childhood. Prayer remained my constant source of strength and clarity as I navigated the ups and downs of teaching. Passion drove me to continuously seek better ways to connect with my students and inspire them. As I witnessed the transformation of young lives in my classroom, it became even more apparent that I was where I belonged.

As I continued to grow in my career, I also learned the importance of persistence, especially on difficult days. There were times when I questioned whether I was making a difference. Those moments of doubt always led to breakthroughs—whether a struggling student finally grasped a concept or a parent sent a heartfelt note. Preparation was crucial to my success, not just in lesson planning but in my professional development. I sought out mentors and continued to hone my skills, knowing that growth was essential for me and my students.

Most importantly, I maintained a positive mindset, even on the toughest days. I reminded myself that every challenge was a bridge and every student was capable of greatness with the proper support and encouragement. I learned to celebrate the small victories and to keep pushing forward, knowing that my work had a lasting impact.

Teaching became more than just a career—it was my calling, a way to live out one of the dreams I had dared to pursue. As I moved from those early days in the classroom to leadership roles in education, I carried with me the lessons from my childhood and the unshakable belief that each of us can achieve extraordinary things when we dream big and remain true to our purpose.

Daring to dream big isn't just a catchy phrase; it's my call to rise above the ordinary and embrace the extraordinary life waiting for you—and me. It's an open invitation to break free from the constraints that may have held us back, chase the dreams that set our souls on fire, and boldly step into the purpose uniquely designed for each of us. When I dared to dream big, I realized I was here for a reason: my aspirations aren't just valid—they're necessary. I recognized the greatness within me, and by doing so, I began to create a legacy that will transcend my lifetime. And the same is true for you.

WHY DREAM BIG?

Dreaming big isn't wishful thinking; it's about owning my worth and stepping into my potential. It's about setting goals that challenge me to grow, evolve, and move beyond the familiar. When I dare to dream big, I declare that I'm ready for the possibilities in life, no matter how audacious they seem. I'm embracing the belief that I can achieve the remarkable, even when the path ahead is uncertain.

HOW I DREAM BIG

As my journey of daring to dream big unfolded, music and worship became essential parts of my story. From a young age, I had a love for music—whether singing in choirs or developing a deep desire for worship. My love for music ignited something in me, and that spark has continued to grow throughout my life.

I was able to grasp the concept of playing the cello, but I always had the desire to play the piano. Over the years, I've bought not just one but two pianos, and I've taken lessons to develop my skills. While I may still be a work in progress on the piano, my heart remains fully committed to mastering this instrument. The learning process reminds me that embracing my values means recognizing that I am worthy of the dreams that stir my heart.

My dreams reflect my purpose and destiny, and I hold on to them with unwavering belief, knowing that every step forward is part of the journey. From childhood to adulthood, I sang in numerous choirs, and each experience enriched my love for worship. I've had the privilege of serving as a worship leader, and on some occasions, I've sung solos that allowed me to connect with God and others profoundly. Through these experiences, I began to see the vision of my future in worship. I imagined leading worship on a larger scale, possibly even producing my own worship CD. That dream is still alive in my heart; I understand that visualization connects where I am now to where I am destined to be.

Setting ambitious goals has always been part of my journey. When I enrolled in the worship studies program at Liberty University, it wasn't just about gaining knowledge—it was about challenging myself to grow in new ways. I didn't shy away from the hard work it required; instead, I embraced it because I knew these skills would open new doors for me. The training I received equipped me with opportunities I could never have imagined. Soon, I traveled to places like India and Africa, where I led phenomenal worship workshops.

In those workshops, I encountered worshipers hungry for God's presence in ways I had never seen before. People were delivered and set free from sickness, depression, and disease simply by being immersed in the presence of the Lord through worship. Witnessing worship in those countries was a life-changing experience, and it deepened my understanding that worship isn't just an act—it's a lifestyle. This realization pushed me further to take decisive action toward my dreams.

As I continue to dream big, I know that resilience is my greatest ally. The road hasn't always been easy, whether learning to play an instrument, overcoming obstacles in my personal and professional life, or pursuing my goal of having a successful business. But I stayed focused on the vision, knowing that every challenge is an opportunity to strengthen my resolve. Even when things don't happen as quickly as I'd like, I keep moving forward, trusting that persistence will lead me to fulfill my dreams.

Cultivating a positive environment has also been critical to my journey. I've surrounded myself with people who believe in my dreams just as much as I do—mentors, fellow worshipers, and uplifting communities encouraging me to keep pressing forward. These connections have been invaluable, especially when I've faced moments of doubt. Drawing inspiration from others who have dared to dream big has shown me that I am not alone in this pursuit. Together, we uplift and empower one another to continue striving for greatness.

Through it all, I take time to reflect and adapt. I celebrate my victories—whether it's a breakthrough in worship or a milestone in my musical journey. I also learned from setbacks that flexibility is critical to realizing my dreams. Sometimes, the path I envisioned looks different in practice, but I remain open to God's leading, knowing He is the source of my strength, and He guides me through every twist and turn.

The dream of producing a worship CD still burns brightly within me, and I know that one day, it will come to fruition. In the meantime, I remain committed to worship as an essential part of my life—a daily expression of my love and devotion to

God. Through prayer, fellowship, and worship, I continue to dream big, trusting that the best is yet to come.

All these steps were instrumental to my journey. I encourage you to use these steps in your own life.

1. **Embrace your value.** Start by knowing you are worthy of the dreams that stir your heart. Your dreams will reflect your purpose and destiny. Hold on with unwavering belief.
2. **See the vision.** Imagine yourself living out your dreams. What does that future look like? How does it feel? The power of visualization helps connect your current state to your future destination.
3. **Set ambitious goals.** Don't shy away from goals that push your limits. These goals will compel you to develop new skills, seize new opportunities, and overcome challenges you never thought possible.
4. **Take decisive action.** Dreams without action are just wishes. Break down your grand vision into concrete, actionable steps and take them with determination. Every step forward is a victory.
5. **Stay resilient.** The road to realizing big dreams is paved with obstacles, but resilience is your greatest ally. Stay focused on your vision and see every challenge as an opportunity to strengthen your resolve.
6. **Cultivate a positive environment.** Surround yourself with people who believe in your dreams as much as you do. Seek mentors, connect with uplifting communities, and draw inspiration from others who've dared to dream big.

7. **Reflect and adapt.** As you progress toward your dreams, reflect on your progress. Celebrate your victories, learn from your setbacks, and adjust your course. Flexibility is crucial in turning dreams into reality.

THE RIPPLE EFFECT OF DREAMING BIG

In essence, let's discuss the ripple effects of dreaming big. Dreamers, be vigilant. The only limits on your dreams are the ones you set for yourself. Along your journey, things can happen that will cause you to get stuck in your comfort zone— that's what happened to me.

At a pivotal point in my life, I no longer pursued my dreams. I felt unfulfilled, trapped in a cycle of procrastination, and completely disconnected from my hidden potential. Self-doubt crept in, whispering that I wasn't worthy of the big dreams I once held dear. Physically, I wasn't taking care of myself—I was overweight, stuck in bad eating habits, smoking cigarettes, and abusing alcohol. Negativity and detrimental habits had gained control, thwarting my ability to live the life I was destined for.

Then, the lightbulb came on in the middle of that struggle. I had an awakening and realized that I needed help. I couldn't keep living this way, feeling stuck and unworthy. So, I decided to seek assistance from various sources. I turned to prayer, reached out to mentors and coaches, sought spiritual counseling, and surrounded myself with people who could lead me in the right direction. This support system became a lifeline, but even then, I knew the hard truth: No one could make the necessary changes for me. I was the one who had to take action. All the external help in the world wouldn't matter unless I were willing to confront the main problem—me.

When we face challenges, obstacles, and setbacks in life, they can cause ripple effects that affect every area of our being. That's what happened to me. But the lesson I learned is that I am the only one who can make the changes needed to break free. No one else can bridge the gap between being stuck in complacency and stepping out to pursue your dreams—you have to decide to do it for yourself.

These are the steps I took that helped me reignite my journey toward daring to dream big:

1. **Clarifying my dreams.** I came to understand my true desires. I needed to unearth the dreams that layers of uncertainty and diversion had concealed.
2. **Cultivating a positive mindset.** I knew that if I was going to change my life, I needed to change my thinking, so I focused on renewing my mind, speaking life over myself, and building my confidence.
3. **Taking action.** Dreams without action are just wishes. I started taking small, deliberate steps toward my goals, even when it felt uncomfortable. Every action brought me closer to my vision.
4. **Embracing courage over comfort.** I realized that staying in my comfort zone wasn't helping me grow. I had to be brave enough to face my fears and step into unfamiliar territory, knowing that courage is what leads to transformation.
5. **Developing my skills and talents.** I am committed to sharpening my gifts. Whether learning new skills, taking courses, or seeking feedback, I invested in my

personal and professional development to show up fully prepared for the opportunities ahead.

6. **Surrounding myself with like-minded people.** I became intentional about surrounding myself with people who inspired, uplifted, and challenged me. Their belief in me strengthened my belief in myself.

7. **Staying persistent and resilient.** Success doesn't come easy—there are setbacks along the way. However, I've trained myself to see each obstacle as a stepping stone. I stayed persistent, trusting that resilience would carry me through every challenge.

8. **Aligning my purpose with my actions.** I ensured everything I did aligned with my God-given purpose. I wasn't just dreaming for the sake of it; I was following my calling and moving in sync with it.

9. **Celebrating small wins.** Every triumph, no matter how small, should be acknowledged and celebrated. Recognizing my progress has been a powerful motivator that has kept me moving forward.

I realized I was the only one holding myself back through this journey. I also learned that I had the power to change that narrative. The same is true for you. When you dare to dream big, you must be willing to face yourself, overcome the obstacles, and step into the life that's waiting for you. It's not easy, but every step you take will bring you closer to the extraordinary.

As I continue to dare to dream big, I don't just transform my own life—I inspire others to do the same. My courage to pursue my dreams sparks a chain reaction, empowering those around me to reach for their greatness. Together, we create a world where more people believe in the power of their dreams and their impact on the world.

So, I challenge you to dare to dream big. Let your vision be your guide, your actions fuel your journey, and your resilience carry you through. The world needs your unique contributions because your dreams can make a difference, not only in your life but also in the lives of many others. If you are struggling, I am here to tell you it's time to break those barriers and step into the abundant life.

To all dreamers: So, you've got that fire inside, ready to unlock your true potential and step into greatness. Utilize these essential steps that can help you dare to dream big and make it happen. Trust me, it's a journey worth taking!

1. CLARIFY YOUR DREAM

Before you can unlock anything, you've got to know what you're after, right? I had to get super clear about my dreams.

Ask yourself:

- What would you chase if nothing could hold you back?
- What lights your soul on fire and makes you feel alive?
- And here's the biggie: How can your dream connect to the legacy you want to leave?

2. CULTIVATE A POSITIVE MINDSET

Your mind is where it all begins. I had to kick self-doubt and fear to the curb—no more letting limiting beliefs stop me. It's all about rewiring your thoughts! Start practicing daily affirmations and surround yourself with positivity. Here's one of my favorites: *I have greatness inside of me that the world needs.*

When you shift your focus to growth and stop chasing perfection, you'll see failure as another step forward.

3. TAKE ACTION ON YOUR DREAMS

It's easy to dream, but the magic happens when you take action. I learned that dreams without action are just fantasies, so here's what I did:

- Break those big, audacious dreams into smaller, bite-sized steps.
- Set SMART (Specific, Measurable, Achievable, Relevant, Time-bound) goals to keep yourself on track.
- Show up every day, even when progress is slow. Trust me, it adds up!

4. EMBRACE COURAGE OVER COMFORT

Growth doesn't happen in your comfort zone. If you want to unlock your true potential, you've got to push yourself past those fears. Ask yourself:

- Where can you be bolder?
- What doubts do you need to confront?
- How can you trust yourself enough to take that leap of faith?

5. DEVELOP YOUR SKILLS AND TALENTS

Your potential is tied to your unique skills and gifts. Invest in them! I'm always learning, whether it's through courses, mentorship, or good ol' self-study.

- Be patient with yourself—growth takes time!
- Seek feedback from people you trust, and never stop refining your talents.

6. SURROUND YOURSELF WITH LIKE-MINDED PEOPLE

The people around you matter. A lot. It would help to have a community that lifts and pushes you toward your dreams. Here's what worked for me:

- Find mentors who inspire and challenge you.
- Build connections with like-minded people who get your vision.
- Distance yourself from anyone who drains your energy. We don't need that negativity.

7. STAY PERSISTENT AND RESILIENT

This is a marathon, not a sprint. There were moments when I wanted to throw in the towel, but persistence kept me going. When things get tricky:

- Remind yourself of your "why." Why did you start this journey? What's the bigger picture?

- Use setbacks as learning opportunities, not reasons to quit.
- Keep showing up. Even if it's a slow crawl, you're still moving forward.

8. ALIGN YOUR PURPOSE WITH YOUR ACTIONS

- Your purpose is the compass guiding you toward your potential. Make sure your actions align with your long-term vision. I always check in with myself:
- Do my goals still match up with my passions?
- How does what I'm doing today bring me closer to the legacy I want to create?

9. CELEBRATE SMALL WINS

- Celebrating the little victories is fuel for your journey. Take time to reflect on how far you've come!
- Reward yourself for every milestone, no matter how small.

These wins will keep you motivated to tackle the next big step. These steps will unlock your potential and start turning those dreams into reality. And the best part? You'll be creating a legacy that will ripple out to future generations. Your dreams matter, and the world is waiting for your offer!

Now, let's get into some necessary habits we need to formulate!

HERE ARE SOME PRACTICAL EXAMPLES OF DAILY HABITS:

- **Start your day with a gratitude list—a game-changer for your mindset.** Growing up in a modest household, I learned to appreciate the little things early on. To this day, I start my mornings by listing what I'm grateful for. Whether it's the roof over my head, the love of my family, or the opportunities I have, gratitude keeps me grounded and opens my heart to more blessings. I've found that this simple habit shifts my perspective, making even the most challenging days feel more manageable.

- **Write down or revisit your goals to stay focused.** When I started my teaching career, I kept my goals in a journal. I wrote about my desire to impact my students' lives, lead in my community, and grow as a worship leader. Revisiting those goals daily kept me motivated, especially when progress felt slow. Now, whether I'm working toward a business venture or preparing for a new venture, I revisit my goals regularly to remind myself why I started.

- **Set one nonnegotiable daily task that moves you closer to your dream.** While working on my piano skills, I made it a point to practice every day, even if it was just for fifteen minutes. That small, consistent action added up over time. The same goes for my spiritual growth—whether reading a scripture or spending time in prayer, I take at least one step forward each day. This discipline keeps me moving toward my dreams, no matter how busy life gets.

- **Practice self-care. our health is essential to your success.** I've learned that I can only thoroughly pour into others if I care for myself. Whether going for a walk, doing water aerobics, cycling, spending time in quiet reflection, or simply ensuring I get enough rest, self-care has become a priority. It's not just about physical health—it's about nourishing my mind and spirit so I have the energy and clarity to pursue my goals.

HOW CAN PERSISTENCE IMPACT YOUR LIFE?

Persistence is the heartbeat of anything you are trying to accomplish. One vivid example was when I first started working with children with disabilities. The early days were challenging and filled with moments of doubt and uncertainty. But every time I pushed through a tough day, I wasn't just learning how to be a better teacher—I was building a habit of resilience that my students and colleagues could look up to. My determination to stick with it, to improve myself, and to serve with passion has become part of the story I leave behind.

Another moment where persistence shaped my life was during my mission trips to India and Africa. Conducting worship workshops with people hungry for God's presence was a transformative experience. There were logistical challenges, language barriers, and moments where things didn't go as planned. But staying the course, pushing through those obstacles, and focusing on the purpose God had placed in my heart resulted in breakthroughs I will never forget. People were delivered, healed, and uplifted. That persistence created ripples that will impact lives for years to come.

Each step, setback, victory—it all adds up. My persistence, whether in my personal life or career, has shown the next generation that greatness doesn't come from giving up. It comes from sticking with it, learning, and growing through trials. I am living proof that if you keep pushing, believing, and daring to dream *big,* you can build a legacy that inspires others long after you're gone. Your dreams are worth it—never stop chasing them! Keep pushing, keep believing, and keep daring to dream *big*!

As I conclude *Daring to Dream Big: Unleashing Your Inner Courage,* this journey has profoundly impacted my life. Looking back at the struggles, the challenges, and even the harsh words spoken against me, I now see that none of it could stop God's destiny in store for me. Through it all, two scriptures have been the foundation that I have leaned on, and they continue to shape my path today: Psalm 91:1–2 and Psalm 37:23–24.

Psalm 91:1–2 reminds me, "He who dwells in the shelter of the Most High will rest in the shadow of the Almighty." No matter the challenges or hardships that I faced, I always felt secure under the protection of God. This scripture became my shield, helping me stay strong, knowing that as long as I remained close to Him, nothing could derail His purpose for my life. In those quiet moments of prayer, I found peace and the courage to keep moving forward, no matter how overwhelming the road ahead seemed.

At the same time, Psalm 37:23–24 became a reminder that "The steps of a good man are ordered by the Lord, and He delights in his way. Though he may stumble, he will not fall, for the Lord upholds him with His hand." This scripture interweaved into my life every season—whether I was questioning my path or facing setbacks, I trusted that God guided my steps. Even when I stumbled, I knew He was holding me up, ensuring my journey wasn't in vain.

Together, these scriptures have been my anchor. They've kept me grounded, helped me persevere, and reaffirmed that every part of my journey—both the highs and the lows—was part of God's more excellent plan for my life. Through faith, I dared to dream big, and because of His promises, I continue to walk boldly into the future He has destined for me.

Dreamers, don't let the naysayers get in your ear. Your journey was predetermined long before you came into this world—before you even existed in your mother's womb, God had already planned your pathway. Your future holds greatness, and nothing negative can alter that destiny. Remember, you are a winner. Never forget who you are and the incredible purpose placed within you. Keep dreaming, keep pushing, and let nothing stand in the way of your destiny!

Meet the Author | Dr. Valarie W. Harris

Dr. Valarie Harris, with an unwavering dedication spanning forty years of experience, has become a notable authority in education, leadership, and personal and professional development. Her perspective transcends geographical boundaries, exemplified by involvement with the missions team for Global Missions in Ghana with endeavors that also extend to disaster relief efforts in Grenada, reflecting her unwavering dedication to humanitarian causes that uplift the underserved and vulnerable.

As an educator, minister, author, director of ministries, speaker, certified empowerment coach, and business consultant, Dr. Valarie leverages her expertise to empower leaders, educators, women, and aspiring entrepreneurs. Her teaching style fuses motivation, guidance, and empowerment, drawing from personal experiences to make content relatable and engaging.

She continues to inspire, encourage and empower individuals to embrace growth and change and pursue their aspirations through her work and writings.

YOUR THOUGHTS

YOUR THOUGHTS

THE COURAGE TO PURSUE: RELEASING YOUR INNER STRENGTH

ZELDA B. LYNCH

"Daring to Dream Big: Releasing Your Inner Strength" is a powerful declaration that every person encounters at some point in their life. It's a universal challenge, an invitation to rise above the ordinary and step into the extraordinary. Some of us will approach this moment, face it head-on, and move through it with a sense of ease, almost as if we are guided by an unseen hand. We set goals, and without even realizing it, we accomplish them, seemingly without effort. For others, however, the journey is not as smooth. There are those of us who struggle, who face obstacles at every turn, and who find it difficult to navigate the path toward our dreams.

And then, there are those times when everything seems to be going perfectly—when our plans are unfolding just as we envisioned, and success appears to be within our grasp. But suddenly, life happens. Unexpected events or challenges arise. Suddenly we encounter the unpredictable storms of life that threaten to derail our progress and shake our confidence. In those moments, it's easy to feel overwhelmed, to want to abandon our dreams and jump ship. But my advice to you is this: Don't jump ship. Stick with your current plan. Keep moving forward. These storms are not the end. They are the beginning of something greater. Remember, every one of us has goals, visions, and aspirations for our lives. And life being life comes with its share of interruptions. The question is, how will you respond. Will you choose to move forward, to press on despite the challenges, or will you allow yourself to be held back?

My suggestion to you is to always choose to move forward. Don't jump ship. Instead, anchor yourself in faith and press on.

From the very moment of your conception, a journey began— your journey. Someone somewhere began making plans regarding your fate. These decisions were made without your input, without your consent, and yet they have shaped the course of your life. Perhaps the person making these decisions considered the possibility of abortion. Maybe they thought about contacting an adoption agency. But then, something miraculous happened. They decided to keep you, to bring you into this world, to nurture and care for you. And in that moment, your life's purpose began to take shape.

Regardless of the choices made, to God be the glory—you are here! God chose you to be here. Your presence on this earth is not a coincidence nor an accident, but it's part of God's divine plan. God's choice was for you to be here, in this moment, with a specific purpose and a unique destiny. He has something special for you to accomplish, something that only you can do in the way He has designed. As it says in Jeremiah 29:11 (NIV), "For I know the plans I have for you," declares the Lord, "plans to prosper you and not to harm you, plans to give you hope and a future." This verse is a powerful reminder that even when times are tough, God is still in control. He has not forgotten you; He knows exactly what you need. His plans for you include restoration, prosperity, and a future filled with hope. Even when it doesn't look like things are going your way, remember that God has already established a future for you. Keep the faith, hold on to hope, and trust that He is still in control.

As a young child, you couldn't make decisions for yourself regarding your future. Your parents or legal guardians took on that responsibility, making plans and setting the course for your life. They began to groom you, to prepare you to be a positive contributor to society. And at some point—perhaps around the age of three—people started asking you that familiar question: "What do you want to be when you grow up?" Do you remember the first time someone asked you that? It might have been an innocent question, but in reality, it planted a seed—a seed of dreaming big, of imagining possibilities beyond your current reality.

As a young child, your dreams were likely grand and bold because your dreams knew no bounds. You allowed your imagination to soar. You had an innocence and a sense of wonder that allowed you to dream without limits. Your dreams might have seemed unrealistic or impossible to the adults around you, but to you, they were completely attainable. You probably shared your dreams with excitement and passion, speaking with such enthusiasm that no one could convince you otherwise. When asked what you wanted to be when you grew up, you envisioned yourself as a superhero, the President, or a famous athlete—no dream was too big or too far-fetched. That innocence, that belief in the impossible, is a powerful gift. It is a reminder that our dreams are meant to be bold and boundless, not confined by the limitations of the world around us. Your parents, recognizing the importance of these dreams, didn't discourage you. Instead, they encouraged you, fostering your imagination and helping you to dream even bigger.

Your parents' ultimate goal was probably to help you become a positive contributor to society, to inspire and encourage you to set goals for yourself. They wanted to assist you in cultivating and fine-tuning your dreams, to mold and prepare you for the future—your future. To that end, they began introducing you to a variety of possible career pathways—perhaps through the arts, sports, or organizations that fostered your interests in science, math, or education. They invested in you, encouraging and nurturing that seed of daring to dream big.

But as we grow older, life has a way of dimming that light. Challenges arise, doubts creep in, and we begin to lose sight of those big dreams. Yet, even when life throws unexpected curveballs—be it financial setbacks, health challenges, or the loss of a loved one—you must remember: This is not the end. God's plan for you remains unchanged. What seems like a setback is often a set up for a greater blessing. "For My thoughts are not your thoughts, neither are your ways My ways, declares the Lord" (Isaiah 55:8, KJV). Trust in His plan even when the road ahead seems unclear. Trust God even when you can't see or trace Him.

Do you remember when you first started to dream big, to set personal goals for your life? Did those dreams seem impossible or unattainable at the time? Perhaps they did, but remember this: God has promised us in His Word that with Him, "all things are possible." In Mark 9:23 (NKJV), Jesus said, "If you can believe, all things are possible to him who believes." Similarly, in Matthew 19:26 (KJV), Jesus said, "With men this is impossible, but with God all things are possible." And in Luke 1:37 (KJV), we are reminded, "For with God nothing shall be impossible." These verses underscore the importance of faith in God. Our God is capable of working in and through any situation, no matter how dire it may seem. Trust in Him, even when you can't see a way forward. He has promised to supply all your needs according to His riches in glory (Philippians 4:19 NIV). Our God is faithful, and He will provide.

Often, when we are daring to dream big, we rely on various tools to help us stay on track. Some of us design vision boards or develop a mental vision of how our dreams will manifest. These vision boards serve as a way to track our progress, to ensure that we are moving toward our goals in a timely manner. We use them to keep ourselves accountable, checking off milestones as we go, making sure everything aligns with our set timeline.

As you track and plan, your dream may seem to be coming into fruition just as you envisioned. But then, something unexpected happens. Life throws a curveball, and suddenly, you lose focus. Perhaps you became a parent or had to care for an elderly family member. Maybe you faced financial setbacks, health challenges, or the loss of a loved one. These unforeseen circumstances can make it seem like your dream is slipping away, like you're no longer on track to achieve it. In those moments, you might wonder what to do next. Should you forget your dream? Should you scale back your ambitions? My advice to you is this: Don't forget your dream. Don't scale back. Continue to move forward! God has a plan for you, and it's bigger than any obstacle in your way. Jeremiah 29:11 reminds us that God's plans are to prosper us, to give us hope and a future. What you may see as a setback or failure, God can use as a blessing, either for you or for someone else. Isaiah 55:8–9 tells us that God's thoughts are not our thoughts, and His ways are not our ways. His wisdom and plans are perfect, even when we can't see them clearly.

When you were creating your vision for your life, remember to include God in the process. Did you seek His guidance and direction? You may have been confident in your plans, but as children of the Most High God, we must remember that He has the final say. Romans 8:28 assures us that all things work together for good for those who love God and are called according to His purpose. Our God is sovereign, and He has the power to arrange events and situations so that the result is beneficial for His believers. Even when things don't look good in the moment, trust that God is working it all out for your good. Hold on to His promises and keep your dreams alive. Continue to review and refine your vision and remember what God has said in His Word: "Write the vision, and make it plain upon tables, that he may run that readeth it. For the vision is yet for an appointed time, but at the end it shall speak, and not lie: though it tarry, wait for it, because it will surely come, it will not tarry" (Habakkuk 2:2–3 KJV).

As you reflect on your life, you realize that you have the capacity to dream and to dream big. But somewhere along the way, you may have lost that zeal, that passion, that excitement. Maybe you lost focus, or perhaps you stopped dreaming big altogether. Have you lost that spark, that drive to dare to dream big? It is easy to lose your zeal, the passion for dreaming big, especially when faced with life's hardships. But ask yourself: What's holding me back?

Many of us didn't lose the desire to dream big, but we have allowed other things—fear, doubt, the opinions or voices of others—to hinder us from moving forward. The fear you feel is not from God. He has promised us in His Word that He did not give us the spirit of fear, but of power, and of love, and of a sound mind (2 Timothy 1:7 KJV). Don't let a lack of confidence, anxiety, or the comfort of familiarity keep you from moving ahead. Don't let these feelings prevent you from achieving those big dreams you have for yourself. Remember, you were created for a purpose, and that purpose is grand. It's time to reclaim your dreams, to reignite that passion, and to step boldly into the future God has designed for you. Daring to dream big is not just about reaching for the stars; it's about trusting in the One who placed those stars in the sky. Your journey is unique, your purpose is divine, and your dreams are worth pursuing with all the courage and faith you can muster.

OVERCOMING AGE AND OTHER OBSTACLES: RELEASING YOUR INNER COURAGE

It's not always fear, anxiety, or life circumstances that hold you back. Sometimes, the barrier is something subtler, something you may not even realize is influencing your decisions—your age. You might be thinking, "I'm too old to start now," or "That ship has sailed." These are the lies that the enemy whispers in your ear, trying to convince you that it's too late, that your time has passed, and that no one wants to hear what you have to say. But I'm here to tell you: STOP LISTENING TO THOSE LIES!

God's calling on your life doesn't expire with age. He has called, appointed, and anointed you for such a time as this. Right now, in this moment, God is allowing things to happen in your life for a reason. Our God is purposeful, and nothing He does is by accident. You may never fully understand how your life impacts others, but trust that it does. Just as the biblical character Esther was placed in a specific position "for such a time as this" (Esther 4:14), so too are you placed exactly where you need to be to fulfill your purpose.

Now, you might be asking, "How do I reignite that zeal, that desire, that passion and excitement for dreaming big and making it happen?" The answer is simple—it begins with God. Matthew 6:33 KJV reminds us, "But seek ye first the kingdom of God, and His righteousness; and all these things shall be added unto you."

When you put God first, everything else falls into place.

So, how do you get your zeal and passion back? Here are some steps to consider:

- **Pray about everything.** Start with prayer. Bring everything to God—your dreams, your fears, your uncertainties. Prayer opens the door for God to move in your life.
- **Place everything in God's hands.** Once you've prayed, leave it with God. Trust Him enough to place your dreams, your plans, and your fears at His feet.
- **Put God at the center of your life.** When you design your vision board or make plans for your future, make sure God is at the center. Place your vision in His hands, and trust Him to guide your steps.
- **Analyze what got you off track.** Be honest with yourself. What caused you to lose focus? What led you

astray? Seek God's wisdom in identifying these obstacles.

- **Ask God to help you get back on track.** Once you've identified what went wrong, ask God to help you realign your life with His plan. He's ready and willing to help you get back on course.

RELEASING YOUR INNER COURAGE

Many people say it's easier said than done. Releasing your inner courage—what does that really mean? Let's break it down. To release something means to set it free, to let go, to loosen it from confinement. When we talk about your "inner" courage, we're referring to something deep within—the core of your being, where your strength resides. Courage, in its truest sense, is the ability to continue moving forward even when the situation seems difficult, painful, or uncertain.

When you're asked to release your inner courage, you're being asked to set free what God has already planted deep inside you. This isn't something you muster up on your own; it's something God has given you. You might think it's impossible, that you don't have the means, the knowledge, or the resources to do what God is asking of you. But remember this: God doesn't call the equipped; He equips the called.

Even if it feels uncomfortable, even if it requires stepping out of your comfort zone, you must move forward. Releasing your inner courage often means doing things that challenge you, that stretch you, and that force you to rely more on God and less on yourself. It's about strengthening your faith, stepping out in faith, and trusting God every step of the way.

What has God placed inside of you that you're still holding on to? What gifts, what anointing, what calling has He placed on your life that you haven't yet released? Are you allowing these God-given gifts to remain dormant inside you? Why haven't you released them yet? Are you letting fear, age, or other people's opinions hold you back? Are you worried about finances, circumstances, or the challenges you might face?

Remember this: God has a perfect plan for your life. His plan is designed to prosper you, to give you hope, and to secure your future (Jeremiah 29:11). The anointing and calling God has placed on your life are not just for you. They are meant to bless others as well. That business idea, that ministry, that dream—whatever it is that God has placed in your heart—was given to you for a reason. Don't let it wither inside you. Draw strength from your inner courage, step out on faith, trust God, and move forward with what He has given you.

We often think we have plenty of time, so we procrastinate. Or we think we don't have enough time because we're too old. But God knows everything about you—your strengths, your weaknesses, your fears, and your doubts. When we procrastinate, we not only block our own blessings, but we also hinder the blessings of others who are connected to our obedience.

So, what's holding you back? Is it fear? Remember, God has not given us a spirit of fear, but of power, love, and a sound mind (2 Timothy 1:7). Is it negativity, whether from others or from yourself? Challenge those thoughts. Are they from God, Satan, or your own self-doubt? Change the narrative. Replace those negative thoughts with positive ones. Speak life over your dreams, and watch how things begin to shift.

Throughout this chapter, we've focused on two main themes: dreaming big and releasing your inner courage. Dreaming big is the easy part. The challenge comes in discerning if that dream is from God, including God in the dream, and then moving forward to bring that dream to fruition. Releasing your inner courage is another challenge, especially if you're trying to do it without God. We often dream big, but we make the mistake of writing our story without God in it. When we allow God to write our story, we see how He takes what we thought were mistakes and turns them into opportunities for blessing. Romans 8:28 reminds us that all things work together for good to those who love God and are called according to His purpose.

When you let God write your story, you must be willing to move yourself out of the way and say, "Lord God, have Your way." You must confront and identify what's holding you back. If you're unsure of what's hindering you, ask God to reveal it to you. Ask Him to show you the root of the problem. Then, ask Him to lead, guide, and direct you in moving beyond those obstacles. Trust Him, and be willing to follow His leadership and instructions.

Let God write your story. Give all those challenges and hindrances that seem impossible or too hard for you to solve to God. Remember, nothing is too hard for God (Genesis 18:14; Jeremiah 32:17; Jeremiah 32:27). Trust Him even when you can't see or trace His hand. In everything, give thanks (1 Thessalonians 5:18). God has a way of turning things around in ways we can't even imagine. When you surrender your dreams, your fears, your life to Him, you open the door for His power to work in ways beyond your comprehension.

So, I ask you again: What's holding you back? It's time to release your inner courage, to step out in faith, and to pursue the dreams God has placed in your heart. Don't let age, fear, or doubt rob you of the destiny God has for you. You were created for greatness, and now is the time to step into it. Dream big, trust God, and release your inner courage. The world is waiting for what you and God have to offer. Only you can fulfill the purpose God has designed specifically for you. Let God write your story! Your story is still being written. And with God as the author, it's going to be a masterpiece.

Meet the Author | Zelda B. Lynch

Zelda Lynch is an enthusiastic encourager, motivator, and educator. Through her journey as an educator, she has had the incredible privilege of impacting lives from infancy to adulthood. What began as a career choice has blossomed into a profound calling, where Zelda educates and serves as a counselor, therapist, motivator, and encourager. Reflecting on this path, she has fully embraced the fact that being an educator isn't just a job—it's a lifelong mission.

Zelda is thankful daily for God's guidance in leading her down this path. Through His grace, Zelda has witnessed how her efforts can uplift others, fostering self-assurance, faith, and a deeper spiritual connection. As Zelda continues this journey, she finds inspiration in guiding people toward their full potential and nurturing their faith.

YOUR THOUGHTS

_____
_____
_____
_____
_____
_____
_____
_____
_____
_____
_____
_____
_____
_____
_____
_____
_____
_____
_____
_____
_____
_____

YOUR THOUGHTS

_____

_____

_____

_____

_____

_____

_____

_____

_____

_____

_____

_____

_____

_____

_____

_____

_____

_____

_____

_____

_____

_____

NAVIGATING FROM UNFORGIVENESS TO FORGIVENESS

MARILYN Y. STEWART

 "Count it all joy, my brothers, when you meet trials of various kinds, for you know that the testing of your faith produces steadfastness. And let steadfastness have its full effect, that you may be perfect and complete lacking in nothing."

— JAMES 1:2–4 ESV

LIFE'S DISAPPOINTMENTS

As we navigate through this thing called life, we will experience many things, both good and bad. The bad experiences sometimes remain in our thoughts longer than the good times. We can have numerous disappointments, and at times, trauma in our lives, which will make us wonder where is God. Why did He allow this or that to happen? When these incidents occur in our lives, it makes it hard to trust God. But, God never promised us that life would be easy or free from hurt. I know it is hard to trust God in all things on occasion, but we must. Can you imagine your life without God? Well, I can't, and I don't want to know what life would be like without Him. We have to learn how to count it all joy and trust God because He has our backs. Proverbs 3:5–6 KJV tells us, "Trust in the Lord with all thine heart, and lean not unto thine own understanding. In all thy ways acknowledge him, and he shall direct thy paths."

Many levels of disappointments hurt deeply, and this is when the unforgiveness comes in. As we know, occurrences like job loss, divorce, being looked over for a promotion, broken relationships, betrayal by someone you trusted, et cetera, are just a few things that will bring disappointment and hurt into your life. Oftentimes, the betrayals in our lives are caused by some event that a person orchestrated from behind the scenes. Once someone has hurt you one way or another, it is sometimes hard to forgive them. If we are honest, we feel that some offenses should never be forgiven. At this point, I am sure that you can think of one or two incidents where we felt that person did not deserve our forgiveness. I can think of a time when I told someone something in confidence, and they couldn't wait to share it, and because they shared it, it caused a disagreement between that person and myself.

In our minds, they committed a crime against us, so we are going to make them pay by not forgiving them. Who are we hurting?

Your unforgiveness could also be associated with some trauma you experienced in your childhood or even your adulthood. We should never minimize or attempt to measure someone else's trauma to ours because no one deals with trauma the same way. Several things could cause a person to be hurt or even damaged, and they may not even realize it. Some people suffer from abuse, be it physical, verbal, sexual, or mental. It could be from neglect or not feeling accepted for the person we are, just to name a few. At times, this forces people to step outside of their norm to gain the attention they are desperately seeking, which may lead to more complications in life. Always know who you are and who you belong to because, at the end of the day, you have to be able to face yourself in the mirror. We have to learn how to manage our emotions to think clearly and stay focused. Never let someone's opinion be the determining factor in your life. I know this is hard because once someone plants that negativity in your mind, it is stuck there if you are not strong enough to ignore it. God has the final say in everything, and He only wants the very best for us.

 "For I know the thoughts that I think toward you, saith the Lord, thoughts of peace, and not of evil, to give you an expected end."

— JEREMIAH 29:11 KJV

MOVING PAST THE DISAPPOINTMENTS OF LIFE

How can we move past life's disappointments? How do we recover from life's disappointments? Let's start by exploring what forgiveness and unforgiveness mean. This should be a good foundation to start with. According to *Oxford Languages*, forgiveness is *the action or process of forgiving or being forgiven.* Taking a deeper look at forgiveness, let's see what the *Greater Good Science Center* has to say. They stated, "That psychologists generally define forgiveness as a conscious, deliberate decision to release feelings of resentment or vengeance toward a person or group who has harmed you, regardless of whether they deserve your forgiveness." According to the *Counseling Directory*, "unforgiveness is when you are unwilling or unable to forgive someone for upsetting you, betraying you or breaking your trust."

In an article titled "Unlocking the Bible Definition of Unforgiveness—A Closer Look," written by Greg Gaines on January 24, 2024, in *Bible Themes,* he stated the following: "Unforgiveness, according to the Bible, is the act of unwillingness to forgive or show mercy towards someone who has offended or hurt us. It is characterized by bitterness, anger, and resentment, and goes against God's command to forgive others as He forgives us."

Now that we have covered forgiveness and unforgiveness, we can move forward to moving past the disappointments of life. First of all, we should cast our burdens and hurts upon Jesus and allow Him to minister in our lives. It is clearly stated in Psalms 55:22 NLT, *"Give your burdens to the Lord and He will take care of you. He will not permit the godly to slip and fall."* Yes, it is hard to trust Him when we have experienced one disappointment after another, but we have to come to the place where we know that God has brought us through past situations, and He will bring us through any situations we may come up against in the present. Just trust Him!

One thing I have learned in my life's journey of more than sixty-plus years is that you have to let go and forgive. Forgiveness—well, at least for me—is very important in overcoming adversities and disappointments. Forgiveness allows a person to move forward and stop looking behind in the rearview mirror. Most importantly, how can we expect God to forgive us for our transgressions if we can't forgive each other? We can't with a clear conscience expect God to forgive us for something when we are unwilling to forgive someone who has wronged us—be it a friend, family member, church member, co-worker, or some random person. We also have to keep in mind that one day, we may need forgiveness from someone, and we would expect for them to forgive us. It is best stated in Mark 11:25–26 KJV how God feels about forgiveness and our relationship with Him: "And when we stand praying, forgive, if ye have ought against any: that your Father also which is in heaven may forgive you your trespasses. But if ye do not forgive, neither will your Father which is in heaven forgive your trespasses."

For us to successfully move forward, start with letting the past go. It is done, there is no do-over. Move on from it and be released from it. Lord have mercy, I don't know how old I was when I finally learned this, but I was up in age. When you stay in the past, you do yourself a disservice because you are harboring ill feelings about a situation in which the person who may or may not have caused you pain or trauma has either forgotten about it or has apologized for it, and they have gone on with their life, and you are still stuck in the past. Even if they do not acknowledge what they did, for your sake and sanity, please just let it go! It's not worth it. When you don't let go and let God, you hold yourself captive by the situation that grieves you. Also, your failure to forgive will keep you from being forgiven. How can you expect God to forgive your transgressions if you aren't willing to forgive your family, friend, co-worker, or some random person for their transgression against you?

When you forgive, God gives you peace and joy. He smiles at you for doing something hard for you to do, but you did it. Now, let's put this disclaimer in place. It can also be said that forgiving does not mean that you have to continue a relationship with the offender. Make it your business to guard your heart. You can only control your behavior. You can forgive an abuser and leave them or forgive the betrayal and still set a boundary. Now, let's be real, just because you forgive a person, it doesn't necessarily mean that you will forget what they did. Still, if the thought comes back, you can move past it because you have forgiven the person. I feel that unforgiveness oftentimes blocks our blessings.

When you forgive, God opens up so many doors for you—doors you weren't even expecting to be opened. He has a way of restoring you and your faith when He allows His glory to come upon you. Nevertheless, you cannot receive His glory without forgiveness.

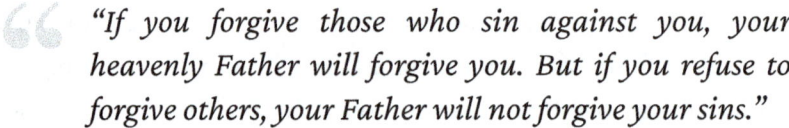

"If you forgive those who sin against you, your heavenly Father will forgive you. But if you refuse to forgive others, your Father will not forgive your sins."

— MATTHEW 6:14–15 NLT

Being able to forgive gave me a new lease on life. It opened my eyes to the freedom of not holding on to stuff from the past. Now, if someone does something to hurt my feelings or disappoint me, I just say it's about them and not about me. As a reminder, people who have a hard time forgiving are not alone. There are plenty of us in the world dealing with this very thing daily. It is human nature.

THE DANGERS OF HOLDING ON TO UNFORGIVENESS

Let's explore the dangers of unforgiveness. I didn't realize the harm I was causing myself by holding on to unforgiveness. My failure to connect the correlation of my mental and physical health to my unwillingness to forgive was mind-blowing. In my mind, they didn't deserve my forgiveness, and I was going to punish them by not forgiving them. Little did I know, that unforgiveness was destroying my life. I was so determined to not forgive that I pushed aside my biblical teachings about forgiveness and my relationship with God. I could not understand why so many of my prayers were going unanswered and then I started wondering where was God. Then, one day, the lightbulb came on, and I realized that I was the cause of my prayers not being answered simply because I chose not to forgive. I was living in sin because I was not acknowledging nor asking for God's forgiveness. I was so caught up in my feelings, that I didn't realize that God was always there! Nevertheless, what is the point of asking for forgiveness when you are unwilling to give forgiveness?

Mentally, we don't realize how unforgiveness affects us. We may not associate bitterness, stress, anxiety, depression, or the need to get revenge with unforgiveness in our lives, but it is a key factor in our mental and physical health suffering. We fool ourselves into believing that what is going on is just a part of everyday life and we will get past it. How can we get past something that we are not facing or acknowledging? We are living in our very own fantasy world. Unknowingly, because we are not facing or acknowledging our unforgiveness, we are creating a prison in our minds by not forgiving. I say prison because we are stuck in the past, and we keep reliving the offense over and over. We are reliving the offense and the person who caused you the hurt or trauma has gone on with their life, and they have probably forgotten all about it. Everyone does not hold on to things, good or bad. If you are in your mental prison by not forgiving, please free yourself and forgive the person or people. You will feel so much better.

Unforgiveness causes us to lose sight of the positive things in our lives because we are so focused on what someone has done to us in the past, and we are still holding on to that hurt. Because of unforgiveness, we are so caught up in our feelings that we do not realize that we are living in disobedience to our Father in Heaven. We have to let it go to align ourselves with our Father in Heaven. Forgiveness will improve our spiritual, mental, and physical health. Forgiveness moves you to a more positive and healthy position in your life. Unforgiveness is not your friend, it is your enemy. It will slowly destroy you from the inside out by causing you to possibly develop health issues. Also, your unforgiveness will allow the devil to get his foot in the door of your life and cause you to make detrimental decisions that you wouldn't have made if you were thinking clearly and not being led by the devil. Don't allow him to enter your life and cause destruction to you or anyone else. As we know, the things that we do out of anger just add to the grief we are already experiencing because our reactions may cause more harm than good. Try to maintain a level head in times of hurt and trauma to eliminate even more hurt feelings and the possibility of not being able to resolve the issue. Trying to pay someone back for something that you feel that they have done to you, oftentimes causes even a larger rift in the relationship.

Stop and breathe before taking any negative actions. Don't allow the devil to control your mind!

THE HEALING PROCESS

The healing comes about when you realize that forgiveness is far better than unforgiveness. Realize that once you let go and let God, He will fight your battles. As stated in Hebrews 10:30 KJV, "For we know Him that hath said, Vengeance belongeth unto me, I will recompense, saith the Lord. And again, The Lord shall judge His people." Let's be frank: Depending on the offense or how often the offense occurred, it isn't always easy to forgive someone. It becomes a challenge to forgive that person, and you feel like it is not worth the effort.

Don't be fooled. It is worth the effort because it is not for them, it is for you. It is for your freedom from holding on to unforgiveness. I know we don't want to hear this, but we are required to forgive no matter what. Let's take a look at what Matthew 18: 21–22 KJV states about this: "Then came Peter to Him, and said, Lord, how oft shall my brother sin against me, and I forgive him? Till seven times? Jesus said unto him, I say not unto thee, Until seven times: but, until seventy times seven." This is a whole lot of forgiveness for one person, wouldn't you agree? However, if we are a follower of God, then we have no choice but to continuously forgive people.

Once I learned that we are all responsible for our deliverance from unforgiveness, I asked God to help me to be able to move past my pain and forgive. We will have to forgive people for the rest of our lives. So, why not make it easy on ourselves? If you are still holding on to the pain of unforgiveness, please ask God to deliver you from that sin. He will do it for you.

Your healing will also include you moving from bitterness, anger, stress, anxiety, and depression to peace, joy, happiness, and most importantly, release from the prison of your mind because of unforgiveness and the pain that you are harboring.

Once you acknowledge the hurt that caused your unforgiveness, then you can find a way to come to terms with the offense and realize that you must move on from it for your sanity. It is important to find a way to move past the hurt or disappointment to gain control of your mental state of mind. You must recognize your emotional state of mind along with your acknowledgment of what caused you the hurt or disappointment because you still have to deal with your emotions to heal. Our emotional state plays such an important part in the healing because we as humans operate on emotions. If we can bring our emotions to a place of peace, then I believe that we can find a way to forgive.

Never forget that we have at some point in time in our life hurt or disappointed someone, and we wanted or expected their forgiveness. So, how could we be so quick to not forgive someone when they hurt or disappoint us? We never want to be placed in a position where someone—or most importantly, God—will not forgive us.

Yes, sometimes it is hard to forgive, but unforgiveness destroys, and forgiveness brings life. We should all want to live our best life, and that includes forgiveness. Keep in mind, that you cannot say you forgive someone and still harbor anger or malice against the offender. You are required to let all of it go.

FINAL THOUGHTS: MOVING FROM UNFORGIVENESS TO FORGIVENESS

When you move from the prison of your mind by not holding on to unforgiveness, you are released from strife, stress, anxiety, depression, bitterness, anger, and vengeance.

Just as a reminder of Mark 11:25, when we don't forgive, we hinder our prayer life with God. As long as we hold on to unforgiveness, we are blocking our prayer life with God. We cannot stand in prayer and ask God for something when we are holding bitterness in our hearts toward someone. Our relationship and fellowship with God are very important, and we shouldn't hinder it with unforgiveness. Face those things that bring you grief and constructively deal with them, and this will propel you to a much better life.

If you have allowed your relationship with God to dwindle because of unforgiveness, take the time and put forth a very strong effort to reconnect yourself with Him by strengthening your relationship and fellowship with Him. Remember, we are all a child of God, and it is required of us to forgive because if we do not, we are sinning against Him.

We must all remember that our self-worth is not based on other people's opinions because everyone is not going to like or love or mean to do good toward us. So, with that said, we must learn to value ourselves and remember who we belong to. There are a lot of deceitful people in the world, and unfortunately, some of them are in our inner circle. You may think that everyone in your inner circle has your best interest at heart, but there are snakes in the pit. Some are jealous of you and are wishing for your downfall. Sometimes, the very people who you do the most for are the very ones who will let you down when you need them (and this could go both ways). When your inner circle disappoints you, the feelings are different. It is more devastating than when a stranger does it. It is heart-piercing. However, you are still required to forgive them, but it may take you longer to recover from the hurt or disappointment, but you are required to do so.

Your healing begins with you, and the road to healing is not always easy, but so worth it. Healing sometimes takes longer than we may want to expect, and it may take even more work than we thought. The result of escaping what is hindering you from progressing in your personal and professional life will make it all worth it. Whereas you have to learn how to forgive, you have to also learn how to ask for forgiveness when you do something to hurt someone. Even if you did not know initially that you hurt them, once they tell you that you offended them, it is your responsibility to ask their forgiveness. Their feelings mean just as much as yours do. Keep in mind that forgiveness goes both ways.

Once we release our sin of unforgiveness, our prayers will no longer be hindered, and God will release so many unexpected blessings because of our obedience. God wants us to dream big, so He can show up and show out in our lives. However, we must keep in mind that this can only occur if we acknowledge our sin of unforgiveness, ask God for forgiveness, and work hard to refrain from unforgiveness. God wants to bless us abundantly and beyond our wildest dreams, so why not do our part for us to truly receive God's best?

Love yourself enough to forgive those who may hurt or disappoint you and to be mature enough to seek forgiveness when you hurt or disappoint someone. Learning your self-worth will encourage you to be the best you can be and recognize that you are a winner. Knowing that you are marvelously made by God is the best reason to want to always be aligned with Him by not being in sin because of unforgiveness. People will be people, and they will sometimes fall short of our expectations, but know that prayer will deliver us from harboring the misdeeds of the person who hurt or disappointed us. God does answer prayers. It is our responsibility to seek God for deliverance from unforgiveness and be willing to allow Him to do the work in us necessary to cleanse us of this sin! It won't be easy, but it certainly will be worth it. Love yourself enough to forgive those who do not value you as the marvelous person you are. Be blessed, and remember to forgive.

MEET THE AUTHOR | MARILYN Y. STEWART

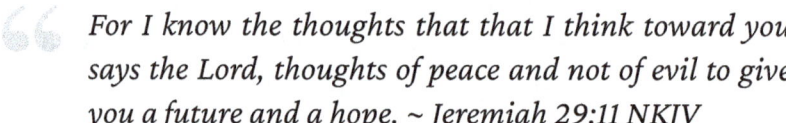 *For I know the thoughts that that I think toward you says the Lord, thoughts of peace and not of evil to give you a future and a hope. ~ Jeremiah 29:11 NKJV*

Marilyn Stewart is a lifelong resident of Virginia and a graduate of Virginia State University with a degree in business administration. She is a member at Mount Olivet Baptist Church, Petersburg, Virginia.

She has been employed with the City of Petersburg for more than forty years, where she has served in several positions. It was during her tenure with the Petersburg Police Department that she was selected to serve on the newly formed board of directors for the Petersburg Police Athletic League in the position of treasurer. It was an honor for her to serve on the board of directors where decisions were made to improve the quality of life for the at-risk children of the city. The success of the program enabled children to experience various activities to which they had not been privy prior because of their economic status. Overall, the children gained different outlooks and developed outlets for positive life-changing experiences.

Marilyn has been working with youths throughout her adult life, having a drawing and open mindedness making her approachable. She was the co-sponsor of the Spirit of Praise Dance Group. The group was favored by God to have the honor and the privilege to perform at numerous churches throughout the tri-city area during their term of operation. Also, Marilyn was an instructor for her church's computer lab ministry, teaching youth beginner classes. She was also the assistant instructor for the senior citizen classes. Marilyn was an assistant for the Judah Dance Camp where she was a facilitator for the mentoring part of the training. She developed a mentoring curriculum titled, *Loving Me Because God Loves Me Best*, which included a journal that was used along with the daily training. Marilyn was the author of a poem developed especially for the Judah Dance Camp titled, "I Am Still Beautiful," highlighting the training module, which was designed to teach the young ladies self-worth by reminding them that they are created by God and loved by God. Marilyn developed the training module for the mentoring part of the camp the following year concentrating on self-esteem and respect.

Occasionally, Marilyn provides inspirational thoughts for her closest friends and co-workers to bring the sun shine into the darkness and also to motivate all to meditate on things of concern in a positive light. And now, here she is working on her very first published writing. God is good!

YOUR THOUGHTS

_____

_____

_____

_____

_____

_____

_____

_____

_____

_____

_____

_____

_____

_____

_____

_____

_____

_____

_____

_____

_____

_____

_____

YOUR THOUGHTS

LISTEN TO WHAT GOD IS SAYING

MALINDA N. WILLIAMS

INTRODUCTION

When I consider the topic of unleashing inner courage, the first place I turn is to the scriptures. Unapologetically, I believe the best way to find inner courage is through what God can provide. While God is the remedy for our troubles, we have the flexibility to create a personalized formula for any given circumstance. Certainly, beneficial "active ingredients" in the formula include a daily quiet time with God and prayer. However, sometimes we may need a dose of encouragement from a favorite scripture or a close friend, much like taking a little extra vitamin C to fight a cold.

As I step out of my comfort zone and embark on a writing journey, this effort is just as much for me as it is for you. Contemplating my future as an author, I realize I must also unbridle my own inner courage. I am absorbing these words and reminding myself to use the daily formula to manifest the fullness of what God is doing, allowing Him to work in me and through me. I trust that the voice I bring will be from unleashed courage given to me by God through faith in Christ with the help of the Holy Spirit! I trust that my message will carry a confidence empowered by the one true living God, whose voice is so powerful, it can move mountains, and whose whisper is so gentle, it reassures me that I am loved, I belong to Him, and He has specific plans just for me.

As His willing vessels, God includes us in the work that He accomplishes in this world. Although He does not need us to achieve anything, He gives us unique opportunities to share in His good work. Oh, how humbling and awe inspiring this is! Like the Old Testament prophet Isaiah, I am undone before God's glory and holiness! What truly matters is serving and pleasing God in our purpose. Therefore, unleashing inner courage is essential for accomplishing our dreams and the specific purpose God has called us to do. Undoubtedly, we need God because there are so many disruptions and adversities that can hinder us from fully actualizing the sustaining courage necessary to accomplish our purpose and the dreams we have dared to dream. Life has its ebbs and flows, and the doses of courage needed may change, but God is the steadiness that counteracts the ocean's tides, helping us to embrace every ripple or tsunami with grace.

With all my love, I trust you will find information herein that will help you unleash your inner courage and benefit you in all of life.

KNOWING GOD AND WHAT YOU MEAN TO HIM

In chapter one of his book, *Knowledge of the Holy*, A.W. Tozer said, "What comes into our minds when we think about God is the most important thing about us." Although this is true of the church as one body, it is also true of each individual believer. With our finite minds, we cannot fully grasp the true fullness of God, however, we can strive to understand His attributes and what the scriptures reveal about Him. This understanding shapes how we live; how we see ourselves; how we relate to others; how we master fear, failures and triumphs; and how we achieve courage and success. The scriptures reveal the promises of God, but we can also consider what God has done for us and others. It is all about God first—who He is—and then there is the impact of God on who we are and how we live.

Knowing God is not about seeking Him for selfish desires, like fame or fortune, but it leads us to live righteously for Him, to put God first in all we do and in every relationship we have. It is about aligning our desires with His and sharing our understanding with others. When we come to the end of ourselves, when we surrender, that is when we are at our very best because then we allow God to work through us and in us. In Matthew 10:39 NIV, Christ said, "Whoever finds his life will lose it, and whoever loses his life for my sake will find it." The world teaches us selfishness, but Christ shows us that true love is found in sacrifice. Christ gave His life for us, and we, in turn, give our lives to Him and to one another. Surrendering to the will of God begins our sacrifice, and it is the best way to experience life with the kind of satisfaction that worldly pleasures can never provide.

I am a recovering worrier, and like an alcoholic, I am living one day at a time and sometimes one minute at a time in a battle to keep a sober mind, not a mind drunk with worry. Being such a worrier, I distinctly remember the moment worry crept into my spirit. It was a warm day, and before a major thunderstorm, I frantically pulled linens off the clothesline in my grandmother's backyard. It was shortly after my grandfather died, and although I am not exactly sure what happened, as a third grader, I started worrying about everything. Growing up in a Christian family, I knew about prayer, so on my knees, night after night, I prayed for my family's protection, and even childishly about protection from the amoeboidal alien monster that grew bigger by absorbing people in the 1958 movie *The Blob*. As silly as it may seem to pray for protection from the blob, thankfully, I knew God was the divine source for help and protection.

Certainly, prayer is an active ingredient that should be constant in our lives, but overcoming worry, or anything else for that matter, requires us to focus on who God is. God is sovereign, omnipresent, omnipotent, omniscient, just, holy, faithful, merciful, loving, gracious, glorious, infinite, and immutable! We must know the Almighty God in our hearts. It is not just an academic knowledge. We experience His love and power through the scriptures and through His involvement in our lives and in the testimonies of others. God is love, we are loved by Him, and He abounds in mercy and grace toward us. Because we know who He is, we can trust Him, and we can confidently lean on Him for comfort, courage, and strength.

However, out of all that we may know about Him and experience through Him, God is still incomprehensible. Even the scriptures often say what He is "like" because it is difficult to rightly and fully articulate who He is. God's full essence is far beyond and greater than the words we use to describe Him. Our finite minds cannot know all there is to know about our infinite God. Since this is the God who also loves us and who cares about everything that concerns us, we have a comfort that can immobilize worry, so that worry does not immobilize us. His greatness is immeasurable, and His love is unfathomable, and with this assurance, we can overcome worry. We can overcome anything.

By embracing the fullness of God, we can fulfill our purpose. Once we understand that the most important thing about our purpose is to please, honor, and glorify God, we can move on to our highest calling, which is to serve Him by serving others. After aligning ourselves with God's call to service, we can tap into what that specifically means for us individually. Our specific purpose often stems from our experiences, talents, and passions. However, what matters is that our desires line up with God's desires, that our purpose lines up with God's purpose for us and that we make a conscious decision to allow God's will to be done in our lives.

We know what is right, what God desires for us, by knowing Him, following His ways, and consulting Him constantly. We must wake up every day, choosing God and His purpose for our lives and accepting the Holy Spirit's direction. We can face every command or request of God, and we can handle every obstacle, triumph, or failure with unbridled strength and courage because we know who God is, and we know that He has our best interest in mind. We must pray with the right heart and motives and never be swayed by our own selfish desires. We must also listen for an answer. Sometimes, we must study and meditate on God's Word until the answer comes, or we must wait for the answer, which might be "no." Sometimes we must prepare ourselves for the answer by allowing God to work in our lives. God may give us small tasks or tall, seemingly insurmountable tasks to prepare us for what comes next.

Knowing God is so much more than what I can express here. The scriptures are filled with truths about His unfailing love, His strength, His faithfulness, His righteousness, His mercy, His grace, His flawless word and perfect ways, and His incomparable great power. In the book of Psalms, God is described as a refuge, a stronghold in times of trouble, a helper to the fatherless, a rock, a redeemer, a fortress, a deliver, and a shield and so much more. It sounds like the psalmists knew God well. Studying God's Word and having a daily quiet time with Him are important parts of the formula to deepen our relationship with Him and profoundly experience His presence in our lives.

On October 21, 2017, six of my family members and I experienced God's mercy, unfailing love, faithfulness, and power as we survived an unbelievable one-car accident to the amazement of a line of onlookers stopped behind us. The rear left tire blew, and the SUV we were in hit several guardrails to slow us down before we flipped over, rolling six hundred feet. I could see and even touch the highway pavement because the window was shattered on the first rollover, and clothes, food, and other items were scattered on the highway. I know God held us all in that SUV because three people had forgotten to buckle up! My brother-in-law who was driving was the only one admitted to the hospital. The rest of us walked away with bruises and cuts, but we often consider what could have happened. Landing back on all four wheels, an off-duty doctor, a nurse, and an emergency medical technician jumped out of their cars to assist us the moment the car stopped rolling. My sister walked around the glass-ridden highway picking up clothes and other items without getting one shred of glass in her bare feet. My glasses were on the highway, but they were perfectly intact. To say the least, God was with us that day and an undeniable truth was evident: God is real. Yes! God is real! His Son, Jesus Christ, is real and so is the Holy Spirit!

We may not be able to explain why certain things happen, like the fact that we survived this accident, when the parents of four young children perished in a car crash on Thanksgiving morning, but we must trust God with all things. He does not love us more than anyone else. We have not done anything remarkable to deserve this mighty blessing, but we have lived to tell everybody that we have experienced God's mercy, power, and love. Our testimonies remind us that we can trust God, and we can lean on Him for help. Trusting God does not mean life will be perfect or easy, but knowing God allows us to walk in His will and in His guidance and to understand that we are never alone, fighting on our own. "Trust in the Lord with all thine heart and lean not unto thine own understanding; in all thy ways acknowledge Him, and He shall direct thy paths" (Proverbs 3:5–6 NIV).

It is also important to understand what we mean to God, so I will start with this familiar scripture, John 3:16 KJV: "God so loved the world that He gave His only begotten Son that whosoever believeth in Him would not perish, but have everlasting life." This scripture lets us know that God is the only one with the power and authority to give the Son who is the only one who could accept and accomplish the assignment —to endure the wrath of God and take upon Himself the punishment for the sins of the entire world, for all people through all of time. The Son was the only one with the power to lay down His life and to pick it up again and to offer us eternal life through belief in Him. What God gave and what Jesus did were born out of a love with a depth that will only be known fully after we reach heaven. So, as much as this scripture speaks to God's power and authority, it also speaks to His great love for us all, a love He lavished upon us in Christ.

Ephesians 1:18–23 and Ephesians 3:16–19 are filled with such richness, they are worthy of great study. However, in these scriptures, the Apostle Paul, a servant of Jesus Christ, told the Ephesians about God's "incomparable great power" and the "exceeding greatness of His power" that is "for us," that is "to us-ward." This is a power so great that it was exerted upon Christ when God raised Him from the dead, seated Him at His right hand, and gave Christ authority over everything. This is the same God who loves us so much that it cannot be measured or comprehended. My brother says God's love is a "phenomenon." We have an inheritance, filled with the riches of God's great power, riches that can strengthen us with courage. We have a love from God that is deeper than the deepest places of the ocean's floor and higher and wider than the expanse of the universe. God's love is greater than what is known or observable by man.

Now consider this, some of it being repeated for emphasis: The same God who created the heavens, the earth, and everything in it; the same God who blew the breath of life into man; the same God whose voice can break the mighty cedars of Lebanon, divide the fires, and shake the wilderness; the same God who gave His only begotten Son; the same Son who died on the cross for the sins of the whole world (stop here and consider the magnitude of that fact); the same Son who was raised from the dead and who was given all authority in heaven and on earth; the same Son who intercedes for us as He sits at the right hand of the Father; the same Son who left the Holy Spirit as our constant Comforter and Counselor...this same God knows everything that matters to us, He knows everything we need, He knows every hair upon our heads, and He calls us the apple of His eye. This same God is mindful of you and me, and He gives us strength and power to unleash our inner courage, a courage that He gives us in the first place! King David said: *"Many, O Lord my God, are the wonders you have done. The things you planned for us no one can recount to you; were I to speak and tell of them, they would be too many to declare"* (Psalm 40:5 NIV). John said: "Jesus did many other things as well. If every one of them were written down, I suppose that even the whole world would not have room for the books that would be written" (John 21:25 NIV). Those scriptures are as true today as they were in the ancient of days. Indeed, you and I are also God's wonders, and Jesus has done many great things for us, far too many blessings to count, remember, or even know. Romans 8:31 tells us, "If God is for us, who or what can be against us?"

When the trials of life are weighing on already burdened shoulders, when difficult decisions loom over the horizon, and when the world seems bleak, dark, chaotic, and unkind, the Holy Spirit is our very present help, reminding us of the great and powerful God we serve. Although His fullness is beyond comprehension, God's love, power, authority, and sovereignty are undeniable, providing all the evidence needed to trust God in every circumstance. My daughter wisely said, "Maybe *we* are all the evidence needed to trust God!"

All may not be right in the world, but everything is all right in God. We know who God is and what we mean to Him! He empowers us to make unleashing inner courage a reality.

KNOWING YOURSELF

A friend recited her first Toastmasters speech to me, beautifully describing her accomplishments, as she dove into the world of public speaking. After she left my office, I found myself wondering what I might say about myself in a three-minute speech. Having been out of college more than thirty-five years, the awards and activities of those days are distant. The most important thing about me was and is that I am a Christian. While being a Christ follower is the most important thing about me, knowing other aspects about my character is essential to fulfilling my purpose and dreams.

Self-reflection or looking in the mirror can be challenging, requiring us to look ourselves squarely in the face and admit shortcomings as well as admirable qualities. However, being real about who we are and how we operate helps us grow and avoid self-imposed obstacles. We will be better people, better contributors, more positive influencers and encouragers, and better servants. We also become better mothers, fathers, children, spouses, friends, co-workers, employees, and business owners. With a strong foundation in knowing God and what we mean to Him, our self-reflection can be thoughtful and purposeful. If we genuinely desire to do God's will, we must be willing to ask ourselves tough questions, to take the time to reflect, and to seek the Holy Spirit's guidance. Through this process, we may discover areas of strength and areas needing change or improvement.

For example, here are ten challenging questions:

- What are my goals?
- Why am I trying to reach these goals —what is my motivation?
- Do I need or want the praise of others, and if so, what am I willing to do to get it?
- How do I handle challenges, obstacles, and failures?
- Do I need additional training to excel in my purpose?
- Am I a procrastinator, and what steps do I need to take to ensure that I meet required deadlines?
- Am I always angry, and what do I need to do about this anger?
- What matters most in my life?
- What am I afraid of?
- What are the obstacles that keep me from completing tasks and goals?

While these are just a few questions, you know yourself best, and you are probably already well aware of the challenges you may face.

Sometimes, we need training, assistance, counseling, mentorships, encouragement, and/or accountability partners to help us overcome obstacles that keep us from reaching our full potential. We are all a work in progress, no matter where we are in our Christian walk, no matter how old we are and no matter how much we have already accomplished in life. As we progress, we can rest assured that God loves us, and He will give us what we need as we diligently seek Him. He will meet us right where we are, strengthening us to be overcomers and more than conquerors—helping us to rise above every obstacle, trial, or distraction, above the naysayers, our shortcomings and selfish desires, and above anything that would hinder our progress as we endeavor to please Him. In essence, self-reflection helps us grow and enhances our Christian walk— "Therefore, my dear brothers, stand firm. Let nothing move you. Always give yourselves fully to the work of the Lord, because you know that your labor is not in vain" (1 Corinthians 15:58 NIV).

Joni Eareckson Tada is a busy Christian author, worldwide speaker, painter, music artist, radio host, wife, and founder of a Christian organization for the empowerment of disabled people in ministry. At the age of seventeen, she became a quadriplegic when she severed her spinal cord after "taking a random and very reckless dive into the shallow waters of the Chesapeake Bay," as she describes it. Afterward, she struggled with bitterness and anger, depression, suicidal thoughts, and self-pity. Eventually, she found solace in God's Word and promises. Although she still had questions about her condition in life, she found contentment in Christ, the one from whom we can receive peace and joy, even in our darkest moments. We may not find answers to every question in our self-reflection, and we may endure adversities in life, but we can still trust God. He can accomplish important work through us despite overwhelming issues, adversities, and afflictions, and despite our flaws and frailties. God gives each of us purpose. It is up to us to decide if we will walk in that purpose.

Sometimes self-reflection will show us that we can walk in those things that we are good at and that we are passionate about. Often that means walking in our God-given talents. In the book *The Element,* Ken Robinson, Ph.D., said, "I believe passionately that we are born with tremendous natural capacities, and that we lose touch with many of them as we spend more time in the world. Ironically, one of the main reasons this happens is education. The result is that too many people never connect with their true talents and therefore do not know what they're really capable of achieving. In that sense, they do not know who they really are." He further indicates, "I use the term the Element to describe the place where the things we love to do and the things we are good at come together." We must revive those things we are good at and passionate about, allowing the fire in our bones to ignite and fuel the flames until they become all-consuming. There will be no room for fear and no time to dwell on afflictions or frailties. Our talents and passions will align with the very purpose for which God made us, and with His help, we will not be able to deny it, conceal it, or hold it in. We can walk confidently in our calling.

The Element highlights successful people who excel because they are doing what they are good at, and they are living out their passions. For instance, Paul McCartney is a successful musician, not necessarily because is he better or smarter than someone else, but because he is living out both his talent and passion. We can add countless others to that list like Michael Jordan, Simone Biles Owens, Michael Phelps, LeBron James, Billy Graham, and Aretha Franklin. Despite adversities, people are often successful because their natural talent and passion give them an edge.

Here are three additional questions for you:

- What is something that I am good at and that I love to do?
- What am I passionate about?

- What can I do every day of my life and it does not feel like a job?

Undoubtedly, God has given each of us a purpose to do something significant—whether it is for the world, our church, or one person in our family or community. I do not know much about Joni Eareckson Tada's husband, Ken, but I feel certain that he has been a significant help in her various accomplishments. For instance, because of her paralysis, Ken pressed on Joni's diaphragm so she could take in more oxygen to sing the high notes of a song she was recording. It is awesome and also mind blowing that a quadriplegic is recording a song, but consider that just maybe Ken's most significant purpose is being a supportive husband, so his wife can evangelize to the world. Although I have seen slightly different versions, one of Charles Dickens' famous quotes says, "No one is useless in this world who lightens the burdens of another." Ken certainly lightens the burdens of his wife, and in doing so, perhaps he also inspires others.

On our life's journey, we can continue to develop our talents and passions while we are cultivating new skills. I have a friend who is a great counselor, and it seems that God is directing her into her purpose, doing something she is already good at and trained to do. However, her purpose is expanding to include group presentations in addition to utilizing her counseling abilities in one-on-one sessions. Public speaking may bring her angst, however, having confidence in what she already knows and remembering to trust God, she will continue to grow and excel in this next phase of her calling.

Oh, how beautiful and uplifting it is to know how important we are to God, but on the other hand, it is not easy to admit we are not perfect people, that we do not have it all together. In our quest to accomplish our dreams and purpose, embracing who we are and who we strive to be is transformative. By honestly reflecting on our strengths and weaknesses, we pave the way for growth, and it enables us to have a clear picture of how to successfully pursue our dreams and purpose. However, in spite of our imperfections, God is able to accomplish his divine purpose in us and through us! (Ephesian 3:20–21 KJV: "Now unto Him that is able to do exceedingly abundantly above all that we ask or think, according to the power that worketh in us, Unto Him be glory in the church by Christ Jesus throughout all ages, world without end. Amen.")

A PEP TALK ON FAILURE AND FEAR

In life, sometimes fierce winds will blow, pushing us so far off course, and all we see is a sea of failure and an atmosphere of fear. However, this does not mean we lose sight of our purpose. Navigating through a storm may require us to slow down, regroup, get a little encouragement, and then to find the inner strength and courage to start again. Often, we must simply wait for the storm to pass to see clearly what lies ahead and which way to go.

Like trials, failures are inevitable in life, but writer and strategist Shane Parrish wisely said, "...it's not the failure that defines your identity, but how you respond." Additionally, renowned writer, poet, inspirational speaker, and activist Maya Angelou said, "Courage allows the successful woman to fail and learn powerful lessons from the failure. So that in the end, she didn't fail at all." While pursuing our goals, it is essential to look back to assess what went right or wrong and to identify any strengths and weaknesses in our plan. Looking back, we can see that a perceived failure became an opportunity to learn something we would not have understood otherwise.

The movie *Apollo 13* gave us a memorable quote: "Failure is not an option." Although often attributed to NASA flight director Gene Kranz, it was scriptwriter Bill Broyles who coined the movie tagline. Looking to understand more about the people of Mission Control, Broyles and fellow scriptwriter Al Reinert talked with Kranz in preparation for the movie. They were especially interested in what happened when things went wrong. Kranz informed them that Mission Control's objective was to plan out all the options, understanding that failure was not one of them, and then to act. Although we aim for success, failures can happen. Sometimes things occur that are out of our control, and sometimes we simply make mistakes. But, if we respond with perseverance and learn from those seemingly unforgiving failures, we have indeed conquered failure.

Known mostly as a longtime president of Morehouse College, Benjamin E. Mays said, "In order to excel, you must first be willing to risk failure." He also said, "It must be borne in mind that the tragedy of life does not lie in not reaching your goal. The tragedy lies in having no goal to reach. It is not a calamity to die with dreams unfulfilled, but it is a calamity not to dream. It is not a disaster to be unable to capture your ideal, but it is a disaster to have no ideal to capture. It is not a disgrace not to reach the stars, but it is a disgrace to have no stars to reach for. Not failure, but low aim is sin."

Benjamin E. Mays was a man of humble beginnings. During the dark days of Jim Crow, he was born in the small town of Ninety-Six, South Carolina, into a family of sharecroppers and former slaves. Although most Black children of southern farmers did not go beyond grade school, Mays' thirst for learning gave him the tenacity to seek and prevail in higher education. He became a mentor to notable men like Martin Luther King, Jr., Andrew Young, and Maynard Jackson. Mays was an influential voice in the birth of the Civil Rights Movement's "intellectual conscience," and as a minister of the gospel, he did not separate his faith from this important work. Imbedded in his life were the lessons from God's Word, his family, and his church, and he was empowered with confidence to live out his passion for education. We can do the same. Through failures and fears, we can find courage in our faith and allow our endeavors to be guided by God.

Like Mays, we all can make a difference in the world. We can all contribute something meaningful, no matter how small it may seem, no matter how many times we fall or miss the mark, no matter how many times we have to crush our fears or step over failures, or whatever the case may be. We keep trying. When God calls us to a specific task, He will certainly help us. Philippians 4:13 NIV tells us, "I can do all things through Christ who strengthens me." Although unknown to us, God often prepares us long before the task is at hand. From an early age, Mays was being prepared to be a spiritual mentor and intellectual father to many. Decades after graduating from Morehouse, former three-term mayor of the City of Atlanta, Maynard Jackson, kept a picture of Mays in his office, a reminder and an acknowledgment of the profound influence Mays had in his life. The influencer Mays became did not happen overnight or without challenges and hard work. Mays kept learning, growing, and moving forward.

Sometimes, we fear failure before we even start, but we must take the risk and dream big, God-honoring dreams. We must reach for the stars although they seem unreachable. When fears and failures push us down on the road to fulfilling our dreams, we can stare them squarely in the face, rise up, and fight another day. After all, we are the children of the Most High God. He will hold us up and give us the strength to keep going no matter what adversities come. Things may not be easy, but easy and cheap are normally not worth it. Taking the risk to make your dreams come true will cost you something, even if the cost is nothing more than time.

Nelson Mandela said, "I learned that courage was not the absence of fear, but the triumph over it. The brave man is not he who does not feel afraid, but he who conquers that fear." Having lived in a time of great turbulence amid apartheid, Mandela spent twenty-seven years of a life sentence in prison. It is easy to consider Mandela's time behind cold, lifeless bars as failure and defeat. It would also be understandable if Mandela had allowed the harsh treatment inside those prison walls and the unrelenting critics on the outside to reduce his life to one of hopelessness, hatred, and failure. However, Mandela did not faint or lose his resolve because he understood that he was doing something more significant than himself. As an attorney, he was prepared to fight using the law for himself and others while in prison. Prison helped him to realize that apartheid lived in the hearts of many, but it had not overtaken the hearts of all. Mandela said, "Prison is itself a tremendous education in the need for patience and perseverance. It is, above all, a test of one's commitment." Mandela did not have a spirit of fear. He had a spirit of fairness, patience, perseverance, and prison was not a consuming failure.

Isaiah 41:10 NIV says, "Fear not, for I am with you; do not be dismayed, for I am your God. I will strengthen you and help you; I will uphold you with my righteous right hand." Recently, my sister was reminded of this scripture in an uncanny way. Among other things, a wristband bearing the scripture repeatedly appeared in her path during a difficult and disheartening situation. God was reassuring her of His presence. Rest assured, God is always with us, even if there is nothing in front of us or falling in our path to remind us.

Jeremiah 29:11 tells us God promises us a future and a hope. I add emphasis to the indelible truth, we can trust God. We can trust that God is fulfilling His purpose for our lives because His desires have become our desires and dreams. Through God, we have a future and hope, so there is no need to fear, to worry or to allow failures to stifle our resolve and purpose. We have hope through Christ and what He has already done for us. If through Christ we have this magnificent thing called eternal life, which is life forever, surely God can help us to crush fear, overcome failures, and rise courageously.

CONCLUSION

We are always changing, growing, and learning, but holding on to God's truths will guide us through every season of life. When we feel discouraged, we find courage in knowing who God is and who we are in Him. Trust that God is always working in every situation, even when we are unaware of His presence. God is sovereign and faithful. Often, He sets things into motion, and it is only with the passage of time that we realize God was preparing us for something important.

I encourage you to remain prayerful and to keep a legacy journal of prayer—of answered and unanswered prayers. It will serve as a beautiful source of encouragement as you reflect on countless blessings. Unanswered prayers will honor the wisdom of God, and in time, you will see the manifestation of blessings from unanswered prayers, for God's glory and for your good.

Do not be surprised if you are right where you need to be, where God wants you to be, doing what God wants you to do— even if you are navigating a tumultuous sea and are fighting to get back on course. Plant God's love deeply in your heart, knowing that He is always with you, Christ is interceding for you, and the Holy Spirit is guiding you. You matter to God, and He wants the absolute best for you. You are God's child, and He has an abundance of power and strength to help you accomplish much, to help you steer the ship as it is tossed about by a fierce storm. You are praying, and you are cultivating and growing your relationship with God. Now, it is time to walk courageously.

Who said you cannot do it? Who said you will not amount to anything in life? Who said you do not have the right education? Who said you are from the wrong side of the tracks, the wrong color, the wrong size, the wrong age? Do not listen to the naysayers. Listen to what God is saying. Look for what God is showing you. Never underestimate your value to the world, no matter what negative things you have been told, no matter what adversities you have experienced, and no matter what trauma you carry with you every day. Do not be paralyzed by worry, fear, failure, setbacks, or anything else, but if these things push you to God, then that is exactly where you should be.

You can make a difference in the lives of others. Even if it is for just one person, your impact is valuable. You are a change-maker and a worthy influencer, however, whatever your purpose, you do not need a following to make a difference. With God, you are the difference. Know who you are and who you are in Christ. Plant this firmly in your heart and mind and let the roots of who you are grow deep and strong. Although conditions collide to create the perfect storm and you struggle against its force, nothing can sway you or stop you from fulfilling your purpose. As you listen to what God is saying, know that is your inner courage. Your formula for success is rooted in Almighty God because He has given you the inner courage to accomplish your purpose and your dreams.

MEET THE AUTHOR | MALINDA N. WILLIAMS

Malinda Williams is a vibrant and active member of her church community, where her passion for God shines through outreach activities and encouraging Bible study and Sunday school lessons. Currently, she is taking a bold step into the literary world as a collaborator in the book, *Daring to Dream Big: Unleashing Your Inner Courage*. This inspiring work marks the beginning of a new chapter in Malinda's life as a published author, and it's just the start!

As Malinda looks forward to retirement, she is gearing up to share even more of her heart through upcoming books of poetry. Deeply rooted in her Christian faith, her writing reflects her unwavering devotion to God and her mission to spread the message of His unfailing love. Malinda believes her life's purpose is to encourage others to experience the boundless love of God, a love generously given to the world through Christ.

Family is a cornerstone in Malinda's life. She is the very blessed mother of two wonderful and loving children, Chase and Jasmaura; a caring mother-in-law to Chrissia; and an affectionate grandmother to Nylah and Osiris. Giving her constant smiles and even deep belly laughs, they are her daily joy, and without question, they are important reasons for her great gratitude. Malinda also treasures her family, including her supportive sisters and brother, Ava, Angela, and LaMar, and the rest of her beloved Young, Williams and Mason family. Although her parents and grandparents have gone home to glory, Malinda honors their memory and the profound impact they had on shaping the person she is today. She admits that she is also blessed by the kindness and encouragement of other special people in her life, like Curtis.

Malinda trusts that her journey is a testament to her fervent faith and love for God and her dedication to her family and community. She continues to inspire others with her words and actions, living out her belief in the transformative power of God's love. Get ready to be inspired by Malinda's courageous spirit and heartfelt writings.

YOUR THOUGHTS

_____
_____
_____
_____
_____
_____
_____
_____
_____
_____
_____
_____
_____
_____
_____
_____
_____
_____
_____
_____
_____
_____
_____
_____

YOUR THOUGHTS

Other Titles by
Dr. Valarie Harris

 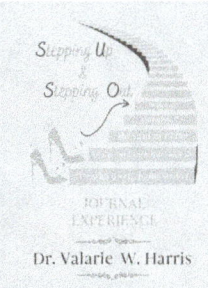